COMPETITIVE RUNNING

WITHDRAWN

RUNNER'S WORLD BEST

COMPETITIVE RUNNING

Edited by Adam Bean,
Runner's World ® **Magazine**

RODALE

This edition first published in 2006 by
Rodale International Ltd
7–10 Chandos Street
London
W1G 9AD
www.rodalebooks.co.uk

© 2006 Rodale, Inc.

Runner's World Best® is a registered trademark of Rodale Inc.

Text Writtem by Sara J. Henry

Interior Photographs: Digital Vision, 68; Brand X Pictures, 76; IndexOpen/Barry Winiker, 71; IndexOpen/LLC, FogStock, 9, 10, 13, 14, 18, 20, 22, 37, 46, 70, 75; IndexOpen/photolibrary.com pty. ltd., 66; IndexOpen/Photos.com Select, 6; IndexOpen/Stewart Cohen, 74; iStockPhoto/Jeannette Meier Kamer, 21; Jupiterimages, 25, 28; Michael Mazzeo, 81, 82, 83, 84, 85, 86, 87, 89, 90, 91, 92, 93; Photodisc, 24, 38, 49; Shutterstock/Chin Kit Sen, 78; Shutterstock/Eduard Cebria, 43; Shutterstock/Felix Fernandez Gonzalez, 30; Shutterstock/Franc Podgorsek, 16, 88; Shutterstock/Galina Barskaya, 65, 72, 80; Shutterstock/Gregory Kendall, 35; Shutterstock/Juan Jose Rodriguez Velandia, 26; Shutterstock/Larry St. Pierre, 33; Shutterstock/ Ljupco Smokovski, 41; Shutterstock/photocay, 52, 58; Shutterstock/Rena Schild, 45; Shutterstock/samantha grandy, 79; Shutterstock/Yusuf Bin Abdol Hamid, 32

Printed and bound in the UK by CPI Bath using acid-free paper from sustainable sources.

1 3 5 7 9 8 6 4 2

ISBN 10: 1-4050-9328-5
ISBN 13: 978-1-4050-9328-6

This paperback edition distributed to the book trade by Pan Macmillan Ltd

Notice
The information in this book is meant to supplement, not replace, proper exercise training. All forms of exercise pose some inherent risks. The editors and publisher advise readers to take full responsibility for their safety and know their limits. Before practising the running programmes and exercises in this book, be sure that your equipment is well maintained, and do not take risks beyond your level of experience, aptitude, training and fitness.

    The exercise and dietary programmes in this book are not intended as a substitute for any exercise routine or dietary regime that may have been prescribed by your doctor. As will all exercise and dietary programmes, you should get your doctor's approval before beginning.

Visit us on the Web at *www.runnersworld.co.uk*

Produced by:
Hydra Packaging, 129 Main Street, Suite C, Irvington, NY 10533, USA
www.hylaspublishing.com

CONTENTS

Introduction

The thrill of competing in an organized race is something every runner should experience.

Perhaps you're completely new to racing, or it has been years since your last competition. Or maybe you've been running short races but are now setting your sights on a half-marathon or marathon. Or maybe you just want to improve your race times and go for a new personal best.

Whatever your status, goals, or motivation regarding competitive running, you'll find the answers you need in this book. We explain how to safely and efficiently increase your distance and speed, how to perfect your running form, how to prepare for bad weather, and how to best fuel your body during training and racing. On top of this we present you with a few additional innovative ways to complement your training.

Part I prepares you for the starting line by supplying you with some of the basic information you need to get you into a competitive mindset. We begin by presenting you with reasons to race, and cover everything you need to know for your first race, including a sample race-day timetable. You'll also find plenty of information on running in extreme temperatures and helpful suggestions for what to wear in cold weather.

In addition, we offer some smart general guidelines as to how and what you should be eating before and during your runs, and finish off the section with a host of valuable racing tips for each specific distance.

Want to be ready for your race in as little as six short weeks? Part II tells you how to do this sensibly, safely, and successfully. This section begins by presenting a list of training principles to follow no matter what plan you've chosen to follow. You'll also learn how to calculate your maximum heart rate and use it as an effective training tool. The majority of

Part II focuses on specific, individualized training plans for four race distances – 5-K, 10-K, half-marathon, and marathon – with separate plans for beginner, intermediate, and advanced runners for each distance. These plans detail a workout for each day of the week, and tell you when to rest. We've also included information on finding a running coach and paying attention to your form, as well as a handy glossary of running terms and their definitions so you can talk the talk.

But there's more to training than just running: what you eat can be of paramount importance, and supplemental training can make a huge difference in your speed and stamina. Part III supplies individual eating plans for each race distance – 5-K, 10-K, half-marathon, and marathon – as well as for each level of expertise. The advice covers everything from breakfast, lunch, and dinner to smart snacks, to what you should eat before and during your event.

This section also includes flexibility training and stretching exercises that will go a long way in keeping your legs and hips limber. Also featured in these pages are several strength training exercises which incorporate nothing more elaborate than a pair of dumb-bells. The exercises will help give you the extra drive you need for the end of a race without limiting your speed and mobility. We conclude with plyometrics – explosive jumping exercises – that will put extra spring into your stride.

Whether you are a newcomer to competitive racing or a seasoned marathon runner, the information and programmes in these pages will have you in shape and mentally ready for your next race. Which race you want to attempt, when you do it and where you choose to run it is up to you.

A word to the wise though, if you are a first-time competitive runner, it is better to slowly get yourself acclimatized by running the shorter distances than dive straight into a marathon. We're not saying you can't do it, but building up gradually will make it seem that much more attainable. Just try to remember the old maxim, slow and steady wins the race.

Now you have all the knowledge you need at your fingertips. The only thing left to do is choose your event and start training. When you line up for your race, you'll be relaxed and ready.

VISUALIZE THE RACE

A common misperception about running is that it is an entirely physical pursuit. The fact is that your mind has a great deal to do with how you train for and run in a race.

Visualization is one tool that competitive runners use to help get them ready for a race. It has been scientifically proven that you can affect your body's muscular response by repeated positive mental images. Just find some time and a quiet space.

One of the things you may want to focus on is imagining yourself running fast and strong. You can take this image and apply it to different aspects of your race such as the last kilometre or a tough hill. Another thing to visualize is the finish line. Many runners do this. If you can see yourself crossing the finish line in your mind, then you can do it on race day.

Whatever you choose to visualize, remember that repetition is key. After the race you will agree that your mind really matters.

PART I:
RACING BASICS

Why Race?

If you haven't yet experienced it, you'll discover that races provide a wonderful energy jolt, from the pre-race preparations, to testing yourself during the run, to the camaraderie you'll experience with the other racers after the event.

Signing up for a race is terrific motivation for getting yourself back into shape.

And you can race at any level, ranging from a casual, local fun run with friends to a marathon in a far-off locale.

Many race events are held each year, and there are as many reasons for racing. Here are just a few.

Meeting people You'll meet people at running races – before, during, and after. You may find new friends, new running partners, or just someone to compete against in the next event.

Boosting your motivation There's nothing like a race looming on your calendar to give your training a boost. If your goal is to increase your distance or improve your speed, an organized run or race can provide all the incentive you need.

Breaking out of a rut Your running has become stale, or you've stopped improving. A race can shake up your routine, inspire you, or give new life to your running.

Competing against yourself It can be difficult to push yourself when running alone, but there's nothing like a starting line and a surge of runners around you to get you going. You may discover a competitive drive you didn't know you had, and may find that you can run harder or faster than you ever dreamed.

Testing yourself Running the same events every year can provide a perfect gauge for your fitness levels. And you'll be able to see how you stack up against others in your age category.

Having an adventure You can choose a race in a place you've always wanted to visit. Plan a year before the race if you want – research the area, plan places to visit, and book well ahead.

Experiencing your own community You may see a new side to your own town or city – your run may take you through scenic or downtown areas you don't normally visit.

Celebrating Turning 40 soon? You've finally kicked a bad habit? Or perhaps a good friend has just recovered from an illness. These are great milestones to celebrate with a race. Mark your special event by competing.

Adding to your t-shirt collection We admit it – we love collecting and wearing t-shirts from running events. These can be good conversation-starters and great to wear while training.

Enjoying the after-race events Many races have festivities and food – and much of the fun of a race is talking it over with other runners after the event.

Your First Race

Yes, lots can go wrong before and during a race. The breakfast you bolted can sit badly on your stomach, and the queues for the portable toilets can be painfully long. You can wear too much or too little, or fail to hydrate enough. To ensure all goes well on the day, plan ahead. Trust us, you'll enjoy the race experience much more if you can hit the starting line calm and well-prepared. The following tips apply to any race distance, but are more important before half-marathons and marathons.

THE DAY BEFORE

Know where you're going If you're heading to a race somewhere unfamiliar, plan the route on a street map or get directions online. Look for pertinent information on your entry form about parking and other details.

Set out your clothing After checking the weather forecast, choose your race clothing accordingly. Overdressing is a common mistake; remember that you will heat up as you run. Here are some basic guidelines:

Above 50° F (10° C): shorts, singlet or short-sleeved t-shirt, suncap, sunglasses.

35–50° F (1.6–10°C): shorts, short-sleeved or long-sleeved t-shirt, lightweight gloves.

Below 35°F (1.6°C): tights, long-sleeved t-shirt and vest or jacket, gloves, hat or earmuffs.

Choose synthetic-blend materials for inner layers, to wick away moisture and prevent chafing. Consider an old sweatshirt or even a heavy rubbish bag with holes cut for head and arms to wear before racing, and discard it at the start of the race.

Pack your race bag Besides carrying extra race clothing in case the weather changes, other items can come in handy:

- Mobile phone (to call home after your race)
- Change of clothes, socks, and shoes
- Energy bars or gels
- Entry form
- Extra shoelaces
- Full water bottle or sports drink
- Lubricant (to prevent chafing and chapping)
- Money

Check the weather on race day and wear layers that you can strip away as you get warmer.

- Race number and safety pins
- Street map
- Sunglasses
- Timing chips, if you've been sent any
- Toilet paper
- Towel
- Water-resistant sunscreen (SPF 15+)

Keep limber A brisk walk or bicycle ride will keep your muscles limber, but you need to avoid warming up too much and tiring them. Exercise for no more than twenty to thirty minutes and at a steady pace. Obviously, this isn't the day to put a new roof on the house or paint your living room.

If you can, it's a great idea to go out and take a look at the course you'll be running.

Review the course If you can drive the course ahead of time, great. Note the location, length, and steepness of hills. If you can't actually travel the course, study the route map and do a mental dress rehearsal. Imagine yourself at the outset of the race, the halfway mark, and approaching the finishing line. Think about goal times for each marker, and how to change your strategy if you're ahead or behind your planned times.

Drink up It is essential to hydrate the day before a race that's long, hot, or both. Aim at 240 ml (8 fl. oz) each waking hour in the last 24 hours, though this doesn't all have to be water. Soup, juice, fruits, and vegetables are good sources, and even cooked pasta is two-thirds water. Make your last beverage of the day juice or a sports drink for the electrolyte content, and stop drinking an hour before bedtime.

Eat wisely Eat plenty of carbohydrates to fill up your glycogen storage tank. Eat an early and relatively light dinner with an emphasis on easily digestible foods such as carbohydrates (pasta, potatoes, or rice) and lean proteins (poultry, fish, or eggs). Steer clear of high-fat and high-fibre foods such as burgers, beans, whole-wheat products, and most dairy products. And now is not the time to sample a new recipe or try out a new restaurant – stick to tried and trusted familiar foods.

Bed check You don't want to enter your race feeling fatigued, so make sure you get to bed at a reasonable hour. Also, whatever you do, remember to set your alarm clock.

ON RACE DAY

Eat lightly Eating on race morning is a balancing act. It's best to have a small, easily digestible, fibre-free meal at least one or two hours before the race. This mini-breakfast might be an energy bar, a bagel smeared with peanut butter, or toast and a banana. Whatever you choose, try it out a couple of times before a hard or long training run to see how your stomach handles it. (In Part III you'll find specific meal advice for each race distance.)

Drink up Consume plenty of water (see p. 24) or a sports drink on race morning. To avoid having a full bladder during the race, stop drinking an hour before the race to give your bladder time to empty itself. If you normally have coffee for breakfast, that's fine.

OVERCOMING RACING ANXIETY

It is not uncommon for even the most accomplished of runners to experience some pre-race anxiety. When you become nervous before a race, your sympathetic nervous system gets the red-alert signal. This fight-or-flight mechanism prepares you for action, but simultaneously, your parasympathetic system, which directs digestion, slows down. Result: if your anxiety levels are high, the undigested food in your stomach may want out. Not fun.

The solution is to eat a light meal that is low in fat, protein, and fibre at least two hours before a race or hard workout. Also, practise relaxation techniques to reduce stress. If throwing up has become a response to hard races or a particular workout, reward yourself every time you finish that event without getting sick. And if you're on the verge of becoming sick, think about a cold, clear mountain stream or something else refreshing.

Distract yourself before the race by starting a conversation with another runner. And remember, you are there to enjoy yourself.

Arrive early Allow yourself enough time to arrive at least an hour before the scheduled start – it may take longer than you realize to park, register, put on your number or timing chip, get in a warm-up jog, and visit the toilet. (The earlier you arrive, the shorter the queue will be – although you may want to schedule a stop somewhere en route.)

Find the right line We're hoping you preregistered, which saves time standing in the registration line, usually some money as well, and gives you a better chance of getting a t-shirt in close to the right size. If not, then head for the registration table. Usually the number pickup is at a different table, and organized alphabetically by your last name. Generally, you pin your race number on your front, using a safety pin on each of the four corners to make sure it won't flap as you're running. Some races use timing chips (sometimes attached to the bottom of your race number or to your running shoes). Read the directions to see where and how to attach them.

Ready, steady, go Warm up gently (see the Race-Day Time-table, opposite). Line up with runners that seem similar in abilities (in marathons they will group you by your mile time) or start near the back. Clear your mind of negative thoughts, think positively, pace yourself, and have fun.

On race day, arrive early, pick up your number, and take your place with your fellow runners.

RACE-DAY TIMETABLE

Here's a sample timetable for a race starting at 9 A.M.:

8:00 Arrive at the start area.

8:00 to 8:10 Visit the toilet before the queue gets too long.

8:10 to 8:15 Apply a lubricant such as Vaseline to protect skin that's vulnerable to chafing and blisters on the toes, feet, inner thighs, and nipples.

8:15 to 8:20 Walk at a moderate clip to begin your initial warmup.

8:20 to 8:30 Accelerate to a jog, or a brisk walk for a marathon.

8:30 to 8:40 Do some light stretches while chatting with friends or mentally reviewing your race plan.

8:40 to 8:50 Strip off your outerwear and leave it in your car or the 'sweats area'. If you choose to wear racing flats, change into them and double-tie the laces.

8:50 to 8:55 Intersperse slow jogging with some 20-second, speedy pickups to prepare your mind and body for the forthcoming race.

8:55 to 9:00 Position yourself in the appropriate pace group if these are designated. If not, line up with the runners who look like they're your speed, or start in the back. (There's nothing as demoralizing as having people flow past you in the first few minutes of the race.) Listen to the announcements. Jog in place, if possible.

9:00 The gun fires. Or not. If the start is delayed, periodically shake your legs loose, jog in place, and stretch lightly while you wait. Once you're up and running, start at a comfortable speed. Pace yourself; it is very easy to get an adrenaline rush at the beginning of a race, and caught up in the crowds cheering you on, which will encourage you to run much faster than you are accustomed to. Stay within your limits and enjoy the event.

Running in Extreme Weather

If you only run on perfect days, you probably will not achieve much distance. If you do not train sometimes in heat and cold, you may struggle when racing under those conditions. Here are some severe weather running tips.

When running in hot weather, be sure to pace yourself, and hydrate often.

SURVIVING THE HEAT

Your body cools you through the evaporation of sweat. It's a reasonably efficient system, but if you don't drink enough fluid to replace that sweat, your run is doomed, and you will be at risk of heat exhaustion or heat stroke as well.

Here are some simple tips to both protect you and help you thrive in hot weather running:

Acclimatize yourself Our bodies are fairly adaptable, and with time can adjust to hot weather. Gradually building your training time in the heat will result in a decreased heart rate, decreased core temperature, and increased sweat output and blood volume. As the weather begins to warm up, try easy, short runs, no more than 30 minutes, at midday and carry some water with you. Gradually increase the distance of those midday runs. As the seasons progress, you'll be building your body's tolerance to heat as the temperatures climb.

Choose cool clothing Select lightweight running clothing with vents or mesh. Microfibre polyesters and cotton blends are good too. Also, wear sunscreen with an SPF of 30+, and consider wearing a hat to shelter your face. Sunglasses are a must.

Avoid dehydration Caffeine, alcohol, antihistamines, and antidepressants can all have a dehydrating effect. Using them just before a run can compound your risk of dehydration. In the case of alcohol, you should avoid it up to one full day prior to a run. Because anti-inflammatories (aspirin, ibuprofen, naproxen) affect kidney function, avoid them before long, hot runs or races.

Drink early and often Top off your fluid stores with 470 ml (16 fl. oz) of sports drink an hour before you head out. Then average another 210–290 ml (7–10 fl. oz) of sports drink about every 20 minutes while running. Sports drinks are preferable to water because they contain glucose and sodium (sugar and salt), which offer three bonuses: they increase your water-absorption rate, replace the electrolytes you lose in sweat, and taste good as well.

Make adjustments Don't schedule long runs or high-intensity runs during the heat of the day. When you run at midday, choose a route that offers some shade. Racing on a hot day, start slower than normal, then gradually speed up. Use the same strategy when the temperature rises during your training runs.

Determine your losses Rehydrate with 470–700 ml (16 to 24 fl. oz) of sports drink for every 0.45 kg (1 lb) of body weight you lose during exercise. Because sweat rates vary enormously, you can get an idea of your own sweat rate by weighing yourself naked before and after a couple of runs. If, for example, you lose 0.45 kg (1 lb) during a 40-minute run, it means you sweated about 470 ml (16 fl. oz) of fluid. You should plan to replenish your fluids at a rate of about 470 ml (16 fl. oz) per 40 minutes of running.

SURVIVING THE COLD

It's easy to err on the side of overdressing during winter, but that can make for a miserable run. Whether racing or training, check the thermometer (and the weather

Hypothermia has been known to occur in temperatures as high as 16°C (60°F), so protect yourself.

forecast) before heading out, and perhaps do a short run close to home or the car so you can discard or add clothing before you set out.

Dress in layers You want to be able to peel off or add layers as the weather changes. The layer next to your skin should be a high-tech polyester that wicks sweat away from your body. One of the key goals of cold-weather running is to avoid the buildup of excess sweat, which often occurs with cotton clothing. Sweat can cause a severe chilling effect if the temperature turns cooler and more windy. Your second layer should be loose and breathable, for example fleece,

with a breathable, wind-resistant, water-resistant windbreaker on top of the other layers. (See Guide to Cold Weather Attire, pages 22–23 for additional information.)

Cover your head During cold weather, you lose up to 50% of your body heat through your head. An appropriate hat – wool or a breathable fabric – is an essential piece of winter running gear. Take it off as you warm up; pull it down as far as you can if it gets colder.

Protect the extremities That means ears, hands, feet and, for men, the penis, and women, breasts. On the coldest, windiest days, be prepared to stuff an extra layer of wind protections or insulation in your shorts or under your running bra. Gloves always provide good coverage for your hands, although mittens don't isolate your fingers as much and will keep them warmer. Protect your feet by wearing a good thick pair (or two) of absorbent socks.

Take care of your face The combination of cold and wind can wreak havoc on your skin. Remember to apply moisturizer and sunscreen to any exposed areas of your face and neck, particularly if the ground is covered in snow. In bitter cold conditions, you may want to use a balaclava (ski mask) or neoprene mask which will provide more complete coverage.

Fuel up adequately Staying well hydrated is just as important in winter as in summer; you're sweating, although you may not notice it. Before or during your run, drink a sports drink or dilute fruit juice, to supply essential fluids and sugars for energy. Also, carry energy bars and gels with you on long runs.

Wear good treads Rain, slush, ice, and snow all make for a slippery surface. Wear good running shoes with a hearty tread, or opt for heavier trail running shoes. But no matter how good a shoe you're wearing, don't press your luck by running on needlessly steep or perilous trails when the weather dictates that you shouldn't.

Although it may feel like you perspire less running in cold weather, you still need to drink plenty of fluids.

Guide to Cold Weather Attire

So, exactly what types of cold weather gear should you be wearing when you go out and brave the elements? There's not just one simple answer to that question. Different temperatures call for different approaches when it comes to clothing. Here are some tips to help you suit up.

MODERATE

4–16°C (40–60°F) – You normally need just one layer of clothing: shorts and short sleeves when the temperatures are on the warm side. On colder days you should think about wearing tights and a long-sleeved top. If it's wet or windy, you might consider a vest and some extras.

Base Layer: Short-sleeved shirt and shorts. For colder weather: lightweight long-sleeved shirt, a pair of lightweight tights

Shell: Water-resistant, wind-proof vest

Essential Extras: Lightweight gloves, headband or hat.

COLD

-12–4°C (10–40°F) – You'll need two layers, and the layer next to your skin (chest, legs and feet) should be a wickable fabric.

Base Layer: Long-sleeved shirt over a t-shirt and medium-weight tights. Tracksuit bottoms or wind pants, vest

Shell: Water-resistant, wind-proof jacket
Essential Extras: Gloves and mittens, headband or hat.

EXTREMELY COLD

-12°C (10°F) and below – Proper layering is key, and you'll probably want to shorten your runs and stay close to somewhere you can take shelter if the weather worsens. It's essential that the layers next to your skin are high-tech wickable fabrics, and that you make sure to protect your extremities.

Base Layer: Long-sleeved shirt, long underwear
Thermal: Fleece shirt. Fleece or medium-weight tights
Shell: Water-resistant, wind-proof jacket and trousers
Essential Extras: Gloves and mittens. Hat or balaclava. Neck gaiter.

These suggestions should serve you well as your regimen hits the winter months. For temperatures colder than the ones listed here, you may want to curtail your running or find an indoor track.

Running in all different types of weather should be part of your race training regimen.

Eating and Drinking for Racing

What you eat and drink during training and the course of the race can dramatically affect how your body responds to the challenge. Here are some helpful nutritional guidelines to follow as you work towards your peak running effort.

A light, low-fat breakfast should be part of your race day training table.

Don't wait to hydrate Drink two 240 ml (8 fl. oz) glasses of water or sports drink two hours before the starting gun. Though you may be the last person in the portable toilet before the start, the water will have passed through your system by that time, and, even better, your body will be primed to accept the fluids you drink during the race.

Select the salty stuff Sports drinks contain sodium, which helps retain fluid and encourages you to drink more. To help get tanked up in advance, reach for a sports drink rather than water. If you don't like sports drinks, have a bagel or a few saltines with your water to get your sodium intake the old-fashioned way.

Eat before you run Take in at least 300 calories – if not a full breakfast – an hour before the start. Be sure you've practised eating the same foods an hour before your long training runs, so that you know your stomach can handle them. This meal will prevent your blood sugar from dropping early in the race.

Choose a prerace pasta dinner Spaghetti is fine. But steer clear of lasagne (which tends to have more fat than carbs, thanks to the cheese) and garlic bread slathered in butter.

Carbo-load, don't fat-load During the last three days, focus on eating carbohydrate-rich foods, such as pasta, potatoes, bread, fruit and fruit juice, low-fat milk and yogurt, low-fat treats, and sports drinks. It's the carbs, after all, not fat or protein, that will fuel you on race day.

Don't eat more the week before Because your training is lighter than normal the week before a marathon, you're burning fewer calories than usual. You need to increase the percentage of your calories that come from carbs, not the amount you eat.

Snack while you stride Long training runs are great for practising refuelling on the go. So pack some pick-me-ups – whether energy bars or gels, sweets, a banana – to munch on along the way. If your body responds by getting

Weigh yourself before and after your runs, and try to replace lost fluids.

pumped, rather than cramped, plan to eat the same things during your race.

Drink as much as you sweat Weigh yourself before and after your long training runs to see how much water weight you lose as a gauge of how much you need to replace en route. For instance, if you lose 1.4 kg (3 lbs) during a three-hour training run, you need to drink an additional 140 ml (48 fl. oz) of fluid during a three-hour race – or 240 ml (8 fl. oz) per half-hour – to keep yourself well hydrated.

Practise drinking The American College of Sports Medicine recommends drinking 150–350 ml (5–12 fl. oz) of fluids every 15 to 20 minutes during a marathon. But that can be a challenge, so practise during your long runs. Just as you can train your body to run longer distances over time, you can teach it to absorb more fluid by gradually increasing the amount you consume in the course of your training.

Choose sports drinks Studies show that marathoners who take in about 200 calories of carbohydrates per hour during long runs or races experience less fatigue and finish stronger than those who don't. If you sip sports drinks at the rate of approximately 150–350 ml (5–12 fl. oz) every 15 to 20 minutes, you'll get plenty of carbs to curb your fatigue.

Eating a carbohydrate-rich dinner the night before a race will give you more fuel for your muscles to burn.

TOO MUCH WATER CAN BE DEADLY

Dehydration can be painful and dangerous, but drinking too much water can also cause a very serious condition – *hyponatraemia,* or low sodium levels. If not recognized, this condition can be fatal.

Typically hyponatraemia occurs on a hot day when you have already lost salt through sweating, and you then drink so much water that you seriously and dangerously dilute your body's sodium content. Symptoms include fatigue, weakness, cramping, nausea, vomiting, bloating and puffiness in the face and fingers, dizziness, headache, confusion, fainting and unconsciousness, as well as pulmonary oedema (fluid in the lungs). Symptoms usually appear late in races, or even afterwards. In extreme cases, it can progress to seizures or coma, and runners in some marathons, including the Boston Marathon in the U.S. have died from hyponatraemia.

Here are some tips to help keep you safe:

- Stick to sports drinks that contain sodium.
- Consider adding salt to your food in the days before a race.
- During the last half of your race, eat some salted pretzels if possible.
- Weigh yourself before and after long runs in various conditions, so you know just how much fluid you lose and how much to ingest. Each 455 g (1 lb) of weight loss = about 480 ml (16 fl. oz) of liquid.
- Skip the salt tablets – the sodium concentration may be so high that it causes vomiting.
- Avoid nonsteroidal anti-inflammatory drugs (such as aspirin, naproxen, and ibuprofen) before or during your race. If you take a pain reliever, an acetaminophen-based one appears to be a safer bet.

Racing Tips

Before beginning any race, it's good to have a short mental checklist of important elements to remember while on the course. Here, we offer you tips for individual races, but you should keep in mind that many of these pointers will apply to just about any distance you run.

Pay attention to your race pace so that you don't go too fast too soon.

5-K TIPS

Consider cushioning The harder your shoe soles, the more your quadriceps have to work to absorb the shock of impact when your feet hit the ground – and the quicker they become tired. Choose a shoe with maximum cushioning as well as a supportive ride.

Warm up Jog for at least 10 minutes prior to the start of the race. A few minutes before the race, do several strides for 50–70 m (55–76 yd). A cold start could make your calves cramp.

Choose your starting spot You may decide to start at the back; it's a lot more encouraging to pass people than to watch them stream by you. If you start with too fast a group, you're likely to start at a pace you can't maintain, and struggle the whole race. Stay within your limits.

Get your results After the race, stay for the awards ceremony and cheer your fellow athletes. Find out your time, no matter where you finished. You'll want to compare it with your 5-K time from the start of your training programme and with later races.

Enjoy the post-race revelry Stick around and mingle. Who knows? You may meet some training buddies for your next 5-K.

Learn from your performance Good race or bad, you can learn a lot. Did you start too fast? Not drink enough ahead of time? Neglect to tie your shoes securely? Wait too long to go into your finishing burst? Look ahead – there are plenty more races to come.

Give it a rest Although you may be raring to go, wait at least two weeks before your next race.

10-K TIPS

Start slowly and carefully. If you're a moderate-pace runner and you start off with the fast pace group, you'll clog up the course and set off faster than you should – and will pay for it later. At the gun, start moving, flowing with the crowd until you can establish your own pace. Keep your hands up to maintain balance, keep your feet low to avoid tripping.

Conserve your energy Slip in behind someone running at a similar pace and, yes, in their slipstream. It's not illegal. It's not even poor form. It's just plain smart.

Save your race-day shoes Once you find a shoe that fits well and feels good throughout your long training runs, take care not to wear it out before the big day arrives. Your best bet: set aside the wear-tested shoes for race day and buy a new pair for your final month of training.

Run an even pace There are several ways to pace yourself in a race, but the most effective is running at an even speed throughout. Use a stopwatch and note the markers around the course to keep yourself on track.

Regroup with a group If you're flagging physically and mentally, run with a group of similarly paced people, even if it means turning up the steam to catch the people up ahead or slowing down slightly to join runners behind you. If you still feel sluggish, go to the front of the bunch and lead the charge. The change of pace and lift you get from leading may be just what you need.

Speed up if you tighten up Stretch out your legs by picking up speed for two minutes tops, then settle back into your former pace. Sometimes a slight pace change is all you need to snap out of a funk. Choose a down-hill stretch if possible, and really lengthen your stride.

Accelerate late You're feeling good and running briskly but within your limits – when should you begin pushing hard? Wait until you've covered 8 km (5 miles) before hitting the accelerator, or

7.2 km (4½ miles) if you're really feeling good. If the race feels tough throughout, save your surge for the final stretch of the course, a short enough distance to help you deal with lactic acid in your leg muscles.

HALF-MARATHON TIPS

Ignore your to-do list Just because you're training less the week before the race, don't fill your downtime with chores. Don't clean the garage. Don't even do your long-postponed filing. Just try to relax.

Scout for tangents You may remember Euclid: the shortest distance between two points is a straight line. Look at the flow of each curve ahead and position yourself so you can take the inside (run the tangent) of the next turn.

Stick to the familiar You don't want to introduce anything unfamiliar on race day. That means wearing the same shoes, the same socks, the same shorts, and the same top you've worn without a hitch on your long runs. And it means eating the same foods and drinking the same fluids you did before and during your most successful long runs.

Race in your training shoes If you wear training shoes during your long runs, your body grows

Pouring water over your head is an excellent way to cool down during warm weather races.

accustomed to running for hours on end in training shoes. If you wear trainers to train, wear them in the marathon – don't switch to seldom- or never-used racing flats. At most, you can gamble with lightweight trainers, but only if you've worn them on several long runs without a problem.

Respect the sun and heat If the weather is sunny, before leaving for the race slather on sun-block, put on a light-coloured hat (it won't absorb the sun, and it will hold the water you pour over your head) and smooth baby oil on your feet to help ward off blisters.

Find your pace, then slow down You know how 8:30s feel in training. But do you know how they feel when your heart's pounding louder than all the feet pounding the pavement? They feel more like 9:30s. In fact, thanks to the race-day adrenaline rush, any pace will feel easier than normal, which could mean you'll go out too fast. Try to pull back until you hit the 8 km (5 miles) mark. Any seconds you lose early are minutes you save later.

Line up loose Fifteen minutes before the start, begin some gentle stretching. Concentrate on the muscles of your calves, hamstrings, glutes, and lower back. Remember, your goal is to start

the race comfortably, so go easy. Keep stretching after you're in the start area. Jog in place to keep your heart rate slightly elevated.

MARATHON TIPS

Study the course Order a video of the race if one is available. Talk to people who've run the race. When you roll into town, drive the course. Cover the whole course, from start to finish, at least once, noting various landmarks and difficult sections so you can visualize your race in detail before you toe the starting line.

Mimic the course If at all possible, train on similar topography as the marathon. Run lots of hills if you're running a hilly marathon, and get used to several hours of flatness if you're running a flat course. If you live in a flat area and are preparing for a hilly marathon, do several runs on a treadmill, altering the incline throughout. If you don't have access to a treadmill, then run on stairways or stadium steps.

Run a dress rehearsal Four or five days before the marathon, do a 3.2–4.8 km (2–3 miles) marathon-pace run in your marathon outfit and shoes. Picture yourself running strong and relaxed. Besides boosting your confidence,

Most races have attendants posted along the course to help direct you.

this run will help you lock in to race pace on marathon day. This exercise will also help keep you relaxed as you wait for the start of your race.

Warm up cautiously At most, jog very easily for about 15 minutes, then stretch your hamstrings, quadriceps, calves, and lower back for another quarter of an hour. With about 15 minutes to go, do a few strides, but no more. You'll warm up plenty early in the race.

Stay calm at the start Try to ignore the electricity coursing through the crush of runners at the line. Take deep, belly-rising breaths to calm your body, relax your mind and supply your muscles with plenty of performance-enhancing oxygen. Close your eyes, visualize a serene, soothing place, and wait there patiently for the gun to go off.

Start slow Run the first 3.2–4.8 km (2–3 miles) 10 to 15 seconds per mile slower than goal pace. This preserves glycogen stores for later so you can finish strong.

Let the weights wait Shelve your usual strength training routine about a month before your marathon, so your legs feel fresh as you approach the big day. Instead, do push-ups, sit-ups, dips, or any exercise in which your body weight provides the resistance to maintain your muscles without sapping your strength.

Wear shorts with a big pocket During the marathon, you may want shorts that allow you to carry an aspirin or two, a few hard sweets, maybe some gels, and maybe your oversized hotel key if you are running outside your home city. Buy the shorts several months before the marathon, and try them out on several long training runs.

Anticipate fatigue You're running 26.2 miles, so it is very possible that your body will protest in some fashion. Prepare yourself by including negative possibilities such as fatigue or muscle tightness when you visualize – and visualize yourself handling any of those troubles when they occur.

Anticipate where you will start your final spurt and finish with dignity.

ART OF THE WATER STATION

The idea is simple – grabbing a cup of water or sports drink from an aid station or volunteer as you run past – but the execution can be less than ideal. If you're not careful, you may end up wearing the fluid you planned to drink or, worse yet, colliding with another runner who has stopped to drink.

Pinch the top As you grab the cup, pinch the top together to make a spout. This keeps water from spilling, and lets you sip from the spout instead of sloshing the liquid all over you.

Never drink anything unfamiliar This is crucial during a long event. Find out in advance what drinks will be at the water stations. If it's an energy drink you've never had, buy some and try it out in conditions similar to race day. A race is the last place you want to try out a new beverage.

Beware of other runners You may have your water stop immaculately choreographed, but your careful planning comes to naught if another runner stops dead in front of you. Assume the worst as you approach water stations, and prepare to dodge slowing or stopped runners.

Drink early, drink often You can save some time by skipping drinking, but this decision can haunt you in the last stage of your race. Unless it's a very short race on a cool day, you're wiser to pause for some liquids.

Research the stations Know ahead of time where the water stations are located, and plan your race accordingly.

Select your stop As you approach the water station, don't head for the first table where every neophyte runner may be stopping; look ahead, and find a less crowded table.

Carry it with you You can certainly walk to drink or stop altogether, but another option is to carry the cup (top pinched together) with you as you run. Drink in small swallows.

Aim high If you're taking a drink from a volunteer, grab the cup high and pinch it as you grab it. Also, you're better off taking a handoff from a volunteer who is jogging along than one who is standing still. Consider basic physics.

PART II:
THE TRAINING PLANS

Basic Training Principles

Training for a race may seem simple: you run harder, faster, and longer. That's true, of course, but to maximize your improvement, maintain your form, and minimize the chances of getting injured, you need to train smart. No matter what event you're aiming at, following these basic guidelines will help ensure that you get to the starting line fit, injury-free and ready to race.

Build a base Whether you're new to running or just increasing your distance or speed, your body needs time to adapt to these new stresses. Building a base of solid distance at a slow, steady speed will prepare your body to handle the stress of faster workouts. Build up to running four to five days a week, with one run at least 45 minutes long. After you have run at this level for several weeks, you will be ready to move on to some more intense workouts.

The specificity rule Your training needs to be specific to the event you plan to run. In short, the most effective training will mimic your race. If you want to run a 5 km (3 mile) road race at a seven-minute-per-mile pace, you need to do some running at that pace. If you're going to race during hot, humid weather, you'll

want to do some training in those conditions. If you want to complete a marathon, you need to do some long-distance runs.

Increase training gradually Sudden increases in distance or training intensity are asking for injury. The 10% rule – increasing your distance no more than 10% a week – will let you safely bump it up. If you're currently running 5 km (3 miles) four times a week for a total of 19.3 km (12 miles), next week you can add 1.9 km (1.2 miles) to your weekly total, increasing each run to 5.3 km (3.3 miles). After increasing your distance for three weeks, hold steady for one to two weeks before increasing again. If you're returning to running after a long break, don't try to start at your previous level; begin at no more than half of your previous weekly distance. The exception to the 10%

rule: if you are starting at less than 16 km (10 miles) per week after a layoff, you can aim at increasing up to 20% a week until you're close to your previous training level. Never increase both speed and distance at the same time. Always increase distance first, then speed.

The hard/easy rule Take at least one easy day after every hard day. Because intense running is more likely to cause inflammation and small tears in your muscles, it's crucial to let your body recover in between hard workouts. A hard day might include a long run, hill workout, intervals, or a speed workout. An easy day can include a slow, short run; no exercise; or cross training such as easy walking, cycling, or swimming. Note: after an especially hard or long work-out, you may need two or more easy recovery days, and always allow at least one day of complete rest per week.

Follow your heart. The most efficient way of training is to moni-tor your heart rate, and exercise at specific intensities, which means percentages of your maximum heart rate. (See Maximum and Target Heart Rate, pages 38–39.) This ensures that you work hard enough to benefit, and helps keeps you from overtraining. In general,

for easy and long runs, work out at 65–75% of your maximum heart rate; for tempo runs (harder than your usual pace), 87–92%, and for intervals, 95–100%. For 5-K races, aim at 95–97%; 10-K races, 92–94%; half-marathons, 85–88%; and marathons, 80–85%.

Training can be a grind, but following these basic principles will make your routine efficient and have you race-ready.

Give yourself a break every once in a while and include some easy runs in your regular routine.

Maximum and Target Heart Rate

An important part of race training is finding your maximum and target heart rate. The maximum rate is the highest at which your heart can beat and feed the body oxygen. The target rate is what you want to maintain while training.

You can find many different formulas for predicting maximum heart rate, and a common one is subtracting your age from 220. If you are 40 years old, your predicted maximum heart rate would be 180 beats per minute.

An alternative formula we have found to be quite effective is to subtract half of your age from the number 205. For instance if you're 40 years old, your predicted maximum heart rate would be 185 (205 minus 20).

Checking your heart rate is also a good way to monitor your training progress.

Or you can monitor your heart rate in a running test:

1. Be sure you're well rested, well hydrated, and well warmed up.

2. Run hard and fast for two to three minutes. Jog back to your starting point. Repeat two more times, running a little harder and faster each time. On the second and last repeat, pretend you're running an Olympic race.

3. Check your heart rate during and immediately after the last repeat. The highest number you see is your maximum heart rate.

You can measure your heart rate with a monitor, which you can buy at any good sporting goods shop. You will wear a lightweight band around your chest and read your heart rate on a wristwatch monitor.

Or you can take your pulse manually. Place your fingers on the opposite wrist and count the beats, or count your pulse by your placing two fingers on your throat, just under your jawline. Using your wristwatch, count for ten seconds and multiply by six. Do this quickly, because your heart rate will start to drop as soon as you stop running.

Next you should consider your target heart rate. There are two common formulas for determining what heart rate to aim at while training. The first multiplies your maximum heart rate x desired training intensity x 1.15. If your maximum heart rate is 185 and you want to train at 70% intensity, your target heart rate would be 185 x 70% x 1.15, which equals roughly 149. You would aim at a heart rate of 149 beats per minute.

The Karvonen formula (developed by Finnish scientist Martti Karvonen for calculating target heart rate for training) incorporates your resting heart rate. This you measure by hand just before you get out of bed in the morning. Subtract your resting heart rate from maximum heart rate, multiply by the desired intensity of training, and then add your resting heart rate back in.

Say you've calculated your maximum heart rate as 185, your resting heart rate is 60, and you want to train at 70% intensity. You'd subtract 60 from 185, multiply by 70%, then add 60:

$$185 - 60 = 135$$
$$135 \times 70\% = 94.5$$
$$94.5 + 60 = 154.5$$

You would aim at a heart rate of 155 beats per minute.

Ultimate 5-K Plan

The 5-K is a great distance for every level of runner. It's manageable enough for first-time racers, and it's the ideal fast short run for seasoned competitors. And you can find a seemingly limitless supply of 5-Ks to compete in. Whether you're a beginner, intermediate, or advanced runner, you can get ready for this race in just six weeks.

BEGINNER

You've been running recreationally two to three times a week for a total of 9.6 km (6 miles) or more, and you may have done a fun run. Now you want to complete a 5-K.

At this stage, your training is simply running: a little more this week than the week before, a tad more the next week. No interval training, no discomfort. Just run.

Every run in this six-week schedule should be a steady run, at an effort that has you breathing comfortably hard, but nowhere close to squinty-eyed wheezing. Enjoy each run. On rest days, hang up your running shoes, but you can take an easy walk, swim, or bicycle ride.

On race day, have a light breakfast such as an energy bar, then arrive early so you can pick up your race number and avoid long queues. Do a little warm-up walking and jogging, sip some water, stretch a bit, and generally

WEEK	M	T	W	T	F	S	S	TOTAL
					THE 5-K PLAN – BEGINNERS			
1	Rest	3.2 km (2 miles)	Rest	3.2 km (2 miles)	Rest	3.2 km (2 miles)	Rest	9.6 km (6 miles)
2	Rest	4.0 km (2.5 miles)	Rest	4.0 km (2.5 miles)	Rest	4.0 km (2.5 miles)	Rest	12 km (7.5 miles)
3	Rest	4.8 km (3 miles)	Rest	4.8 km (3 miles)	Rest	4.8 km (3 miles)	3.2 km (2 miles)	17.6 km (11 miles)
4	Rest	5.6 km (3.5 miles)	Rest	5.6 km (3.5 miles)	Rest	Rest	3.2 km (2 miles)	14.4 km (9 miles)
5	Rest	6.4 km (4 miles)	3.2 km (2 miles)	5.6 km (3.5 miles)	Rest	5.6 km (3.5 miles)	3.2 km (2 miles)	24 km (15 miles)
Taper	Rest	6.4 km (4 miles)	3.2 km (2 miles)	Rest	3.2 km (2 miles)	Rest	5-K Race	

hang out and stay stress-free until the start. Remind yourself that your goal is to finish, to run the whole way, and to finish feeling tired – but not trashed.

INTERMEDIATE

You've been running consistently for at least a year and have run in a few races. You've done a little interval training. You have run a 5-K race. Now you want to step up your training and improve your finishing time.

You'll need to add more weekly distance, and add intensity in the form of timed intervals and a weekly hill-training session. Hill training greatly improves leg strength, aerobic capacity, stride length, and ankle flexion, which lets you 'pop' off the ground

Respect your fellow runners: if you want to pass someone make sure there's room to do so.

THE 5-K PLAN – INTERMEDIATE							
WEEK	**M**	**T**	**W**	**T**	**F**	**S**	**S**	**TOTAL**
1	Rest	6x400 m (437 yd) PI	3.2–8 km (2–5 miles), easy	Hills, 5–8 min	Rest	3.2–8 km (2–5 miles), easy	6.4–9.6 km (4–6 miles), easy	27.3–40.2 km (17–25 miles)
2	Rest	2x800 m (875 yd) PI, 2x400 m (437 yd) PI, 2x200 m (219 yd) PI	3.2–8 km (2–5 miles), easy	Hills, 5–8 min	Rest	3.2–8 km (2–5 miles), easy	6.4–9.6 km (4–6 miles), easy	27.3–40.2 km (17–25 miles)
3	Rest	2x800 m (875 yd) PI, 2x400 m (437 yd) SI, 4x200 m (219 yd) S	3.2–8 km (2–5 miles), easy	Hills, 6–9 min	Rest	3.2–8 km (2–5 miles), easy	8–11.2 km (5–7 miles), easy	30.5–40.2 km (19–25 miles)
4	Rest	2x800 m (875 yd) PI, 1x800 m (875 yd) SI, 2x400 m (437 yd) SI, 2x200 m (219 yd) SI	3.2–8 km (2–5 miles), easy	Hills, 6–9 min	Rest	3.2–8 km (2–5 miles), easy	8–12.8 km (5–8 miles), easy	30.5–45 km (19–28 miles)
5	Rest	2x800 m (875 yd) SI, 4x400 m (437 yd) SI, 4x200 m (219 yd) SI	3.2–8 km (2–5 miles), easy	Hills, 7–10 min	Rest	3.2–8 km (2–5 miles), easy	9.6–14.4 km (6–9 miles), easy	33.8–48.2 km (21–30 miles)
Taper	Rest	4x400 m (437 yd) SI, 4x200 m (219 yd) SI	3.2–8 km (2–5 miles), easy	Rest	3x200 m (219 yd) SI, 3x150 m (164 yd)SI, 6x100 m (109 yd)SI	Rest	5-K Race	

Easy runs: You should be breathing hard but still able to chat while running. For 9:00 pace, use the lower number eg, 3.2 km (2 miles); for 7:00 pace, move toward the higher eg, 8 km (5 miles).

Hills: For 9:00 pace, use the lower number; for 7:00 pace, move toward the higher.

Pace intervals (PI): If your 5K goal is 10:00 pace (31:02 finishing time), run pace intervals at 1:15 (for 200m/219yd), 2:30 (400 m/437 yd), 5:00 (800 m/875 yd). For 9:00 goal pace (27:56), it's 1:07 (200 m/219 yd), 2:15 (400 m/ 437 yd), 4:30 (800 m/875 yd). For 8:00 pace, (24:50), it's 1:00 (200 m/219 yd), 2:00 (400 m/437 yd), 4:00 (800 m/ 875 yd). For 7:00 pace (21:44), it's 0:53 (200 m/219 yd), 1:45 (400 m/437 yd), 3:30 (800 m/875 yd). For recovery, slowly jog half the distance of the repetition (for example, 200 m/219 yd jog after 400 m/437 yd repetitions).

Rest: No running at all. You can walk, cycle or swim if you do it casually.

Speed intervals (SI): For 10:00 pace, run 1:11 (for 200 m/219 yd), 2:22 (400 m/437 yd), 4:44 (800 m/875 yd); for 9:00, it's 1:04 (200 m/219 yd), 2:08 (400 m/437 yd), 4:15 (800 m/875 yd); for 8:00, it's 0:56 (200 m/219 yd), 1:53 (400 m/437 yd), 3:45 (800 m/875 yd); for 7:00, it's 0:49 (200 m/219 yd), 1:38 (400 m/437 yd), 3:15 (800 m/875 yd). For recovery, jog equal distance (for example, 400 m/437 yd jog after 400 m/437 yd repetitions).

more quickly. A scientific study found that running up even a slight hill at a steady pace raises your heart rate up to 26 beats higher than the same effort on the level surface.

On days when you run hills or do intervals, jog 3.2 km (2 miles), then run 4x100 m (109 yd) strides to get primed before the workout; jog 3.2 km (2 miles) to cool down.

Run the first half of the race slower than the second half. Start passing runners at the midway point, as long as you can do so without uncomfortably hard effort.

Increase gradually to discomfort in the last kilometre. In the final 400 m (437 yd), pick it up.

ADVANCED

You have run seriously for at least several years, follow a year-round schedule, have run many races at various distances, and have done regular interval training.

Two words define your training goal: 'race feel'. To race your best, you must mimic in training how it feels to run that far that fast. This means timed repetitions both at and faster than your 5-K goal

If you're just starting or getting back into competitive running, the 5-K is an ideal race.

WEEK	M	T	W	T	F	S	S	TOTAL
			THE 5-K PLAN – ADVANCED					
1	Rest	2x1,200 m (1,312 yd) PI, 2x800 m (875 yd) PI, 4x100 m (109 yd) S	6.4–9.6 km (4–6 miles), easy	2x800 m (875 yd) SI, 2x400 m (437 yd) SI, 4x200 m (219 yd) SI	Rest	6.4–9.6 km (4–6 miles), easy	11–14.4 km (7–9 miles), easy	45–54.7 km (28–34 miles)
2	Rest	10x300 m (328 yd) PI, 4x100 m (109 yd) S	6.4–9.6 km (4–6 miles), easy	2x1,200 m (1,312 yd) SI, 1x800 m (875 yd) SI, 2x400 m (437 yd) SI, 4x200 m (219 yd) SI	Rest	6.4–9.6 km (4–6 miles), easy	11–14.4 km (7–9 miles), easy	45–54.7 km (28–34 miles)
3	Rest	2x1,200 m (1,312 yd) PI, 2x800 m (875 yd) PI, 2x400 m (437 yd) PI, 4x400 m (437 yd) S	6.4–9.6 km (4–6 miles), easy	2x800 m (875 yd) SI, 4x400 m (437 yd) SI, 4x200 m (219 yd) SI	Rest	6.4–9.6 km (4–6 miles), easy	13–16 km (8–10 miles), easy	46.6–56 km (29–35 miles)
4	Rest	3x800 m (875 yd) SI, 4x100 m (109 yd) S	6.4–9.6 km (4–6 miles), easy	3x800 m (875 yd) SI, 3x400 m (437 yd) SI, 3x200 m (219 yd) SI, 2x100 m (109 yd) S	Rest	6.4–9.6 km (4–6 miles), easy	13–16 km (8–10 miles), easy	48–58 km (30–36 miles)
5	Rest	2x1,200 m (1,312 yd) PI 2x800 m (875 yd) PI 2x400 m (437 yd) PI 2x200 m (219 yd) PI	6.4–9.6 km (4–6 miles), easy	4x400 m (437 yd) SI 4x300 m (328 yd) SI 4x200 m (219 yd) SI 4x100 m (109 yd) S	Rest	6.4–9.6 km (4–6 miles), easy	13–16 km (8–10 miles), easy	50–59.5 km (31–37 miles)
Taper	Rest	2x400 m (437 yd) SI 2x300 m (328 yd) SI 2x200 m (219 yd) SI Full Recovery 6x100 m (109 yd) S	4.8 km (3 miles), easy	4x200 m (219 yd) SI 4x100 m (109 yd) S	Rest	3.2 km (2 miles), easy	5-K Race	

Easy runs: You should be breathing hard but still able to chat while running.
Pace intervals (PI): For 8:00 pace (24:50 finishing time), run 1:00 (for 200 m/219 yd), 1:30 (300 m/328 yd), 2:00 (400 m/437 yd), 4:00 (800 m/875 yd), 6:00 (1,200 m/1,312 yd). For 6:00 pace (18:38), run 0:45 (200 m/219 yd), 1:07 (300 m/328 yd), 1:30 (400 m/437 yd), 3:00 (800 m/875 yd), 4:30 (1,200 m/1,312 yd). For recovery, jog a quarter the distance of the repetition (for example, 100 m/109 yd jog after 400 m/437 yd repetitions).
Rest: No running at all. You can walk, cycle, or swim if you do it casually.
Speed intervals (SI): For 8:00 pace, run 0:56 (200 m/219 yd), 1:19 (300 m/328 yd), 1:52 (400 m/437 yd), 3:44 (800 m/875 yd), 5:38 (1,200 m/1,312 yd). For 6:00 pace, run 0:41 (200 m/219 yd), 1:01 (300 m/328 yd), 1:22 (400 m/437 yd), 2:44 (800 m/875 yd), 4:08 (1,200 m/1,312 yd). For recovery, jog half the distance.
Strides (S): Gradually pick up speed to 90% effort, hold that for 18 m (20 yd), then decelerate. Do four to six repetitions of 80–100 m (87–109 yd) after Wednesday and, or Saturday runs.

pace, with short recovery. Because in a race you have no recovery time. The more intimate you become with the race itself, the more you can handle the 5-K's physical and mental challenges on race day. Days when you run hills or do intervals, jog 3.2 km (2 miles), then run 4x100 m (109 yd) strides to get primed before the workout; jog 3.2 km (2 miles) to cool down after, then stretch.

HOW TO FIND A RUNNING COACH

Want some help with your running (aside from this book, that is)? Coaching isn't just for elite athletes. Here are some options.

Running clubs If you can find a running club in your area, chances are there's a coach as well who can help guide you to your personal best.

Charity team coach Many charity organizations have fund-raising teams, and offer coaching and team training sessions. You'll also be raising funds for a needy charity and increasing awareness for that cause along the way.

Personal trainer If you need one-on-one attention, a personal trainer may be right for you. It's not cheap, however. Consider splitting the cost and training attention with a friend or two with common running goals, if the trainer is amenable.

Online coach You can do just about everything else online, and yes, you can find an online coach. Scheduling of course is easy, and you can communicate frequently with your coach. Search for 'online running coach'. Costs vary.

Computer programme Load the programme and you're off. It will ask your current fitness level and goals, and will offer specific training programmes, and often places to log your workouts and even what you eat. Offered by PC Coach, Crosstrainer, and many others. (Search using the words running, training, and software.) Download a trial programme to try before purchasing.

Ultimate 10-K Plan

Training for a 10-K includes the three core components of distance running: strength, stamina, speed. It's not only a great race distance, but you can use it to prepare for everything from the 5-K to the marathon. Remember that these are not one-size-fits-all plans, so if you can't complete a given workout, don't needlessly push yourself. Rearrange training days to fit your schedule as needed.

For some runners, thinking of a 10-K as two 5-K races helps them mentally handle the distance.

BEGINNER

You've been running at least six months and may have done a 5-K or two. You run 5–8 km (3–5 miles) three or four days a week, have done a little fast running, and now you want to enter and race in a 10-K.

Your goal is to run the whole race, so you're going for endurance. You'll do the majority of your running at a steady, moderate pace. We're also going to add some speedwork, which will hasten your transition to the intermediate level. Every week, in addition to steady running, you are also going to do aerobic intervals and some gentle pickups.

In the aerobic intervals, you'll stay well short of going anaerobic (gasping for breath). Treat these

			THE 10-K PLAN – BEGINNER				
WEEK	M	T	W	T	F	S	S	TOTAL
1	Rest	3.2 km (2 miles), 4x1:00 AI, 3.2 km (2 miles)	4.8 km (3 miles) or Rest	6.4 km (4 miles) + 3 GP	Rest	8 km (5 miles)	Rest	25.7–32 km (16–20 miles)
2	Rest	3.2 km (2 miles)	4.8 km (3 miles) or Rest	6.4 km (4 miles) + 3 GP	Rest	8.8 km (5.5 miles)	5.6 km (3.5 miles)	27.3–34 km (17–21 miles)
3	Rest	3.2 km (2 miles). 4x1:30 AI, 3.2 km (2 miles)	4.8 km (3 miles) or Rest	7.2 km (4.5 miles) + 3 GP	Rest	9.6 km (6 miles)	6.4 km (4 miles)	30–35 km (18.5–22 miles)
4	Rest	3.2 km (2 miles), 6x1:30 AI, 3.2 km (2 miles)	4.8 km (3 miles) or Rest	7.2 km (4.5 miles) + 6 GP	Rest	10.4 km (6.5 miles)	7.2 km (4.5 miles)	32–38.6 km (20–24 miles)
5	Rest	3.2 km (2 miles), 4x2:00 AI, 3.2 km (2 miles)	3.2 km (2 miles)	Rest	3.2 km (2 miles), 2 GP	Rest	10-K Race	

Aerobic intervals (AI): Push the pace just a bit, breathing a little harder, followed by slow jogging until you feel rested enough to resume your regular tempo.
Easy runs: You should be breathing hard but still able to chat while running.
Gentle pickups (GP): Gradually increase your pace over 100 m (109 yd) to about 90% of all-out, hold it there for 10–20 m (10.9–21.8 yd), then gradually decelerate. Walk to full recovery before you start the next one.
Rest: No running at all. You can walk, cycle, or swim if you do it casually.

runs like play. Try to recreate that childhood feeling you had running to the park. The gentle pick-ups should be just hard enough to give your body a taste of what it feels like to run fast.

INTERMEDIATE

You've been running a year or more and have done some 5-Ks or maybe even a 10-K. But you've usually finished feeling as if you could have done better. You're ready to train a bit more to see how fast you can go.

You'll be adding distance to your endurance-building long run until it makes up 30% of your total weekly distance, and you'll do a substantial amount of tempo running to elevate your anaerobic threshold. Regular sessions at a little slower than 10-K pace – at tempo-run pace – will significantly

THE 10-K PLAN – INTERMEDIATE

WEEK	M	T	W	T	F	S	S	TOTAL
1	Rest	3.2 km (2 miles), 1 or 2x10-10, 3.2 km (2 miles)	6.4 km (4 miles)	1x400 m (437 yd) PI, 1x800 m (875 yd) PI, 1x1,200 m (1,312 yd) PI, 1x800 m (875 yd) PI, 1x400 m (437 yd) PI	Rest	6.4 km (4 miles), 4x100 m (109 yd) S	9.6–11 km (6-7 miles)	38.6 km (24 miles)
2	Rest	9.6 km (6 miles), incl. 6:00 TUT	6.4 km (4 miles)	1x1,200 m (1,312 yd) PI, 2x800 m (875 yd) PI, 4x200 m (219 yd) PI, 4x200 m (219 yd) SI, 4x100 m (109 yd) S	Rest	7.2 km (4.5 miles), 5x100 m (109 yd) S	11–12.8 km (7–8 miles)	41.8 km (26 miles)
3	Rest	3.2 km (2 miles), 2 or 3 x 10-10, 3.2 km (2 miles)	6.4 km (4 miles)	1x800 m (875 yd) PI, 1x1,200 m (1,312 yd) PI, 1x800 m (875 yd) PI, 2x400 m (437 yd) SI, 4x200 m (219 yd) SI	Rest	8 km (5 miles), 6x100 m (109 yd) S	11–12.8 km (7–8 miles)	43.4 km (27.5 miles)
4	Rest	9.6–11 km (6-7 miles) incl. 8:00 TUT	6.4 km (4 miles)	1x1,200 m (1,312 yd) SI, 1x800 m (875 yd) SI, 2x400 m (437 yd) SI, 2x200 m (219 yd) SI, 4x100 m (109 yd) S	Rest	8 km (5 miles), 6x100 m (109 yd) S	12.8–14 km (8–9 miles)	46.6 km (29 miles)
5	Rest	3.2 km (2 miles), 3 or 4 x10-10, 3.2 km (2 miles)	6.4 km (4 miles)	1x800 m (875 yd) SI, 4x400 m (437 yd) SI, 4x200 m (219 yd) SI, 1x800 m (875 yd) SI, 4x100 m (109 yd) S	Rest	9.6 km (6 miles), 6x100 m (109 yd) S	12.8–14 km (8–9 miles)	49.8 km (31 miles)
Taper	Rest	800 m (875 yd) SI, 2x200 m (219 yd) SI, 400 m (437 yd) SI, 2x200 m (219 yd) SI 6x100 m (109 yd) S	6.4 km (4 miles), 4x200 m (219 yd) SI, 4x100m (109 yd) S	Rest	4.8 km (3 miles) easy, 3x100 m (109 yd) S	10-K race		

Easy runs: You should be breathing hard but still able to chat while running.

Pace intervals (PI): Run at 10-K goal pace to improve efficiency and stamina, and to give you the feel of your race pace. For 10:00 pace (a 1:02:06 10-K), run 2:30 (for 400 m/437 yd), 5:00 (800 m/875 yd), 7:30 (1,200 m/1,312 yd). For 9:00 pace (55:53), run 2:15 (400 m/437 yd), 4:30 (800 m/875 yd), 6:45 (1,200 m/1,312 yd). For 8:00 pace (49:40), 2:00 (400 m/437 yd), 4:00 (800 m/875 yd), 6:00 (1,200 m/1,312 yd). Afterward, jog half the interval distance to recover.

Rest: No running at all. You can walk, cycle, or swim if you do it casually.

Strides (S): Over 100 m/109 yd, gradually accelerate to about 90% of all-out, hold it there for 5 seconds, then smoothly decelerate. Walk to full recovery after each.

Speed intervals (SI): Run these at 30 seconds-per-mile faster than goal pace. For 10:00 pace, run 2:22 (for 400 m/437 yd), 4:44 (800 m/875 yd), 7:06 (1,200 m/1,312 yd). For 9:00 pace, 2:08 (400 m/437 yd), 4:16 (800 m/875 yd), 6:24 (1,200 m/1,312 yd). For 8:00 pace, 1:53 (400 m/437 yd), 3:45 (800 m/875 yd), 5:38 (1,200 m/1,312 yd). Afterward, jog half the interval distance to recover.

10-10s: 10-minute tempo repeats at 30 seconds per mile slower than 10-K goal pace; 3- to 5-minute slow jog after each.

Total uphill time (TUT): Run repetitions up the same hill, or work the uphill sections of a road or trail course.

Cycling is the perfect low-impact workout for your training rest days.

improve both your endurance and running efficiency. You will notice the difference.

Your tempo work includes weekly '10-10s', with intervals and uphill running, all of which strengthen your running muscles, heart, and related aerobic systems.

Running fast requires effort, and some discomfort. But if you find that you can't maintain the same fast pace throughout a given workout, or if your body is complaining loudly, call it a day. Strongly consider adjusting your pace next time.

Realize that one of the most common mistakes is going out and running your first 10-K too fast. On race day, strive for a relaxed, even pace, even if the first half of the race feels too easy.

	**THE 10-K PLAN – ADVANCED**
WEEK	**M**	**T**	**W**	**T**	**F**	**S**	**S**	**TOTAL**

WEEK	M	T	W	T	F	S	S	TOTAL
1	Rest	2x1,200 m (1,312 yd) PI, 2x800 m (875 yd) PI, 4x400 m (437 yd) PI, 6x100 m (109 yd) S	6.4–9.6 km (4–6 miles)	2x800 m (875 yd) SI, 4x400 m (437 yd) SI, 4x200 m (219 yd) SI, 4x100 m (109 yd) S	Rest or 4.8–6.4 km (3–4 miles) easy	6.4–9.6 km (4–6 miles), 6x100 m (109 yd) S	12.8–16 km (8–10 miles)	51–59 km (32–37 miles)
2	Rest	2x1,200 m (1,312 yd) SI, 1x800 m (875 yd) SI, 1x400 m (437 yd) SI, 1x200 m (219 yd) SI, 6x100 m (109 yd) S	6.4–9.6 km (4–6 miles)	4x200 m (219 yd) SI, 4 LS, 4x100 m (109 yd) S	Rest or 4.8–6.4 km (3–4 miles) easy	8–11 km (5–7 miles), 6x100 m (109 yd) S	12.8–16 km (8–10 miles)	53–61 km (33–38 miles)
3	Rest	2x1.6 km (1 mile) PI, 1x1,200 m (1,312 yd) SI, 1x800 m (875 yd) SI, 1x400 m (437 yd) SI, 6x100 m (109 yd) S	6.4–9.6 km (4–6 miles)	4x200 m (219 yd) SI, 4 LS, 4x200 m (219 yd) SI, 4x100 m (109 yd) S	Rest or 4.8–6.4 km (3–4 miles) easy	8–11 km (5–7 miles)	14–17.7 km (9–11 miles)	54.7–63 km (34–39 miles)
4	Rest	2x1,200 m (1,312 yd) SI 1x800 m (875 yd) SI, 1x400 m (437 yd) SI, 1x200 m SI 6x100 m (109 yd) S	6.4–9.6 km (4–6 miles)	5–7 LS, 6x100 m (109 yd) S	Rest or 4.8–6.4 km (3–4 miles) easy	8–11 km (5–7 miles), 6x100 m (109 yd) S	14–17.7 km (9–11 miles)	56–63 km (35–39 miles)

ADVANCED

You've been a serious runner for several years; you've run many races, perhaps even a marathon. You're familiar with fartlek and intervals, and can run comfortably for more than an hour. But now you want a seriously respectable time, and you're willing to work hard to achieve it.

The basis of 10-K training for intermediates is the tempo run. But what you need are short intervals at 5-K and 10-K race pace, which can produce huge improvements over tempo runs. You'll not only improve more, but you'll improve faster, and fortunately you will have run the distance to do these intervals.

THE 10-K PLAN – ADVANCED								
WEEK	M	T	W	T	F	S	S	TOTAL
5	Rest	2x400 m (437 yd) SI, 1x800 m (875 yd) SI, 1x200 m (219 yd) SI, 1x800 m (875 yd) SI, 6x100 m (109 yd) S	6.4–9.6 km (4–6 miles)	9.6–12.8 km (6–8 miles)	Rest or 4.8–6.4 km (3–4 miles) easy	8–11 km (5–7 miles) 6x100 m (109 yd) S	16–19 km (10–12 miles)	58–64.3 km (36–40 miles)
Taper	Rest	1x1,200 m (1,312 yd) m SI, 1x800 m (875 yd) S, 2x400 m (437 yd) SI, 4x100 m (109 yd) S	Rest	4x200 m (219 yd) SI, 4x100 m (109 yd) S, 4x200 m (219 yd) SI, 4x100 m (109 yd) S	Rest	4.8 km (3 miles) easy, 3x100 m (109 yd) S	10-K Race	10-K Race

Easy runs: You should be breathing hard but still able to chat while running.
Lactate sessions (LS): Run about as fast as you can for 1 minute, followed by 3 to 4 minutes of slow jogging.
Pace intervals (PI): For 8:00 goal pace (49:40), run 2:00 (for 400 m/437 yd), 4:00 (800 m/875 yd), 6:00 (1,200 m/1,312 yd). For 7:00 pace (43:28), do 0:53 (200 m/219 yd), 1:45 (400 m/437 yd), 3:30 (800 m/875 yd), 5:15 (1,200 m/1,312 yd). For 6:00 pace (37:15), it's 0:45 (200 m/219 yd), 1:30 (400 m/437 yd), 4:30 (1,200 m/1,312 yd). Recovery is a 1–minute jog (after 400 m/437 yd reps), 2:00 (800 m/875 yd), and 3:00 (1,200 m/1,312 yd).
Rest: No running at all. You can walk, bike, or swim if you do it casually.
Speed intervals (SI): For 8:00 goal pace, run 1:53 (for 400 m/437 yd), 3:45 (800 m/875 yd) 5:38 (1,200 m/1,312 yd). For 7:00 pace, do 0:49 (for 200 m/219 yd), 1:38 (400 m/437 yd), 4:53 (1,200 m/1,312 yd). For 6:00 pace, it's 0:41 (200 m/219 yd), 1:22 (400 m/437 yd), 2:44 (800 m/875 yd), 4:08 (1,200 m/1,312 yd). Recovery is jogging half the interval distance (for example, 400 m/437 yd jog after 800 m/875 yd rep).
Strides (S): Over 100 m/109 yd, gradually accelerate to about 90% of all–out, hold it there for 5 seconds, then smoothly decelerate. Walk to full recovery after each. Strides aren't meant to tire you out, but will add zip to your legs.

You're going to run medium-long on Tuesdays, short and swift on Thursdays. And your steady pace will maintain your vital aerobic base.

For speed intervals and pace intervals, run 3.2 km (2 miles) easy plus four 100 m (109 yd) strides before each session, and 3.2 km (2 miles) easy afterward.

For race day, be sure to know the hills and turns of your 10-K race route, so you can match your efforts to the course. It is also in your best interests to familiarize yourself with the last part of the course (approximately the last 1.5 km/0.93 miles) intimately. You'll want to know exactly where the finish line is so you can plan things out and start your final push at the right time. When and where you start your finishing kick will primarily depend on how much you have left in your tank. Just stay relaxed and finish with dignity.

Ultimate Half-Marathon Plan

The half-marathon (13.1 miles) offers a worthy distance challenge, without requiring the training concentration required by the marathon. This distance is perfect for competitive runners because it can build stamina for shorter, faster races, and improve endurance for a marathon later. You can also recover much faster from a half-marathon – a week compared to a month or more for a marathon.

Running a half-marathon is an excellent tune-up event for the marathon itself.

BEGINNER

You have been a runner for at least a year, but you haven't competed in many races. You can run 5 miles (8 km) at a time without distress, average 15–20 miles (24–32 km) a week, and finished a 5-K, perhaps even a 10-K. Now you want to

WEEK	M	T	W	T	F	S	S	TOTAL
				THE HALF-MARATHON RACE PLAN – BEGINNERS				
1	Rest	2 mi (3.2 km), 5–7x1:00 AI, 2 mi (3.2 km)	Rest	4 mi (6.4 km) + 4 GP	Rest	3–4 mi (4.8–6.4 km)	6–7 mi (9.6–11 km)	19.5–21 mi (30–33.8 km)
2	Rest	2 mi (3.2 km), 5–7x1:00 AI, 2 mi (3.2 km)	Rest	4 mi (6.4 km) + 4 GP	Rest	3–4 mi (4.8–6.4 km)	6–7 mi (9.6–11 km)	19–21 mi (30–33.8 km)
3	Rest	2 mi (3.2 km), 2x[1:00, 1:30, 2:00] AI, 2 mi (3.2 km)	Rest	4 mi (6.4 km), incl. 4x1:00 AI + 5–6 GP	Rest	5K race	4–5 mi (6.4–8 km)	22–24 mi (35.4–38.6 km)
4	Rest	3 mi (4.8 km), 3x[2:00, 2:30] AI, 2 mi (3.2 km)	Rest	5–6 mi (8–9.6 km), incl. 4x1:30 AI + 6 GP	Rest	3–4 mi (4.8–6.4 km)	7–8 mi (11–12.8 km)	24–26 mi (38.6–41.8 km)
5	Rest	3 mi (4.8 km), 3x[2:00, 2:30] AI, 2 mi (3.2 km)	Rest	5–6 mi (8–9.6 km), incl. 4x1:30 AI + 6 GP	Rest	3–4 mi (4.8–6.4 km)	7–8 mi (11–12.8 km)	24–26 mi (38.6–41.8 km)
6	Rest	3 mi (4.8 km), 2x2:00 AI, 2x2:30 AI, 1x3:00 AI+6 GP, 2 mi (3.2 km)	Rest	5–6 mi (8–9.6 km) + 4 GP	Rest	10K race	4 mi (6.4 km)	27–30 mi (43.4–48 km)
7	Rest	3 mi (4.8 km), 2x[2:00. 3:00, 4:00] AI, 2 mi (3.2 km)	Rest	6 mi (9.6 km), incl. 4x2:00 AI + 6 GP	Rest	5–6 mi (8–9.6 km)	9–10 mi (14.4–16 km)	32–34 mi (51.5–54.7 km)
8	Rest	3 mi (4.8 km), 2x[2:00. 3:00, 4:00] AI, 2 mi (3.2 km)	Rest	6 mi (9.6 km), incl. 4x2:00 AI+ 6 GP	Rest	5–6 mi (8–9.6 km)	9–10 mi (14.4–16 km)	32–34 mi (51.5–54.7 km)
Taper	Rest	2 mi (3.2 km), 4x1:00 AI	Rest	2 mi (3.2 km) easy, 4 x GP	Rest	2 mi (3.2 km)	Half-marathon race	

Aerobic intervals (AI): Push the pace just a little. Find a tempo that feels somewhere between comfortable and working a bit. Don't run too hard. Trying to add too much intensity while you're also increasing distance will lead to injury. When you finish, jog very slowly until your breathing returns to normal, then work back into your regular pace. On all other days, just run your assigned distance as you feel.
Gentle pickups (GP): At the end of your run, walk for several minutes, then slowly increase your leg turnover on a flat stretch for 100 m/109 yd (the straight section on a track) until you start to breathe hard. Hold it there for 10–20 m (11–21.8 km), then gradually slow down. Walk to full recovery before you start the next one.
Rest: No running at all. You can walk, cycle, or swim if you do it casually. **Mi:** distance in miles

run for longer, and you are more concerned with finishing than with your time.

First, you'll incrementally increase your weekly distance and long run, which translates into more endurance so you can run more than two hours at a time. You'll also do gradually longer runs at faster than your normal pace to build up your stamina and keep you strong over the last third

						THE HALF-MARATHON RACE PLAN – INTERMEDIATE			
WEEK	M	T	W	T	F	S	S	TOTAL
1	Rest	1x1,200 m (1,312 yd) PI [400 m/437 yd], 2x800 m (875 yd) CI [200 m/219 yd], 4x200 m (219 yd) SI [200 m/219 yd]	3–4 mi (4.8–6.4 km), or rest	2x2 mi (3.2 km) PI [800 m/875) + 4x100 m (109 yd) S	Rest	4 mi (6.4 km) + 4x100 m (109 yd) S	8–9 mi (12.8–14.4 km)	26–30 mi (41.8–48.2 km)
2	Rest	1x1,200 m (1,312 yd) PI [400 m/437yd], 2x800 m (875 yd) CI [200 m/219 yd], 4x200 m (219 yd) SI [200 m/219 yd]	3–4 mi (4.8–6.4 km), or rest	2x2 mi (3.2 km) PI [800 m/875 yd] + 4x100 m (109 yd)S	Rest	4 mi (6.4 km) + 4x100 m (109 yd) S	8–9 mi (12.8–14.4 km) (include 4:00 TUT)	26–30 mi (41.8–48.2 km)
3	Rest	2x1,200 m (1,312 yd) CI [600 m/656 yd], 800 m (875 yd) CI [400 m/475 yd], 400 m (475 yd) SI [200 m/219 yd]	2 mi (3.2 km)	3 mi (4.8 km) + 4x100 m (109 yd) S	Rest	5-K race	6 mi (9.6 km)	24 mi (38.6 km)
4	Rest	2x1–mi (1.6 km), CI [800 m/875 yd], 6x200 m (219 yd) SI [200 m/219 yd]	3–4 mi (4.8–6.4 km), or Rest	4 mi (6.4 km) PI [800 m/875 yd], 1 mi (1.6 km) CI + 6x100 m (109 yd) S	Rest	5 mi (8 km) + 6x100 m (109 yd) S	10 mi (16 km), incl. 6:00 TUT	28–32 mi (45–51.5 km)
5	Rest	2x1–mi (1.6 km) CI (800 m), 6x200 m (219 yd) SI [200 m/219 yd]	3–4 mi (4.8–6.4 km), or Rest	4 mi (6.4 km) PI [800 m/875 yd], 1 mi (1.6 km) CI + 6x100 m (109 yd) S	Rest	5 mi (8 km) + 6x100 m (109 yd) S	11 mi (17.7 km)	28–32 mi (45–51.5 km)

of the race. Two of your running days a week will be challenging, including aerobic intervals and gentle pickups; these will improve your stamina, leg speed, running efficiency, and make your normal pace feel more comfortable. This up-tempo running also adds variety to your training. If you can handle it, include some uphill running on Thursdays.

On race day, start at the back of the pack, and run slower than you think you should for the first few miles. It's easy to get an adrenaline rush at the start. Stay comfortable. Work your way into a controlled rhythm, and stop at every aid station. Drink plenty, eat a little, rest (but no more than 30 seconds), and stretch your legs.

INTERMEDIATE

You have a solid aerobic base. You have been running consistently for several years, have tried various kinds of speed training, average 25–30 miles (40–48 km) a week,

THE HALF-MARATHON RACE PLAN – INTERMEDIATE

WEEK	M	T	W	T	F	S	S	TOTAL
6	Rest	2x800 m (875 yd) SI [400 m/437 yd], 400 m (427 yd) SI [200 m/219 yd], 200 m (219 yd) SI [200 m/219 yd], 1,200 m (1,312 yd) PI		4 mi (6.4 km) (incl. 6x1:00 SI) + 4x100 m (109 yd) S	Rest	10-K race	8 mi (12.8 km)	30 mi (48.2 km)
7	Rest	2x1,200 m (1,312 yd) CI [600 m/656 yd], 4x400 m (437 yd) SI [200 m/219 yd], 4x200 m (219 yd) SI [100 m/109 yd]	3–4 mi (4.8–6.4 km), or Rest	4 mi (6.4 km) PI [800 m/875 yd], 1x800m (875 yd) CI [400 m/475 yd], 2 mi (3.2 km) PI	Rest	6 mi (9.6 km) + 6x100 m (109 yd) S	11–12 mi (17.7–19 km), incl. 8:00 TUT	32–36 mi (51.5–58 km)
8	Rest	2x1,200 m (1,312 yd) CI [600 m/656 yd], 4x400 m (437 yd) SI [200 m/219 yd], 4x200 m (219 yd) SI [100 m/109 yd]	3–4 mi (4.8–6.4 km), or Rest	4 mi (6.4 km) PI [800 m/875 yd], 1x800 m (875 yd) CI [400 m/437 yd], 2 mi (3.2 km) PI	Rest	6 mi (9.6 km) + 6x100 m (109 yd) S	6 mi (9.6 km)	32–36 mi (51.5–58 km)
Taper	Rest	4x400 m (437 yd) CI [200 m/219 yd], 2x200 m (219 yd) SI [100 m/109 yd]	2 mi (3.2 km) PI + 4x100 m (109 yd) S	2x400 m (437 yd) CI [200 m/219 yd], 1x200 m (219 yd) SI	Rest	3 mi (4.8 km) easy	Half-marathon race	

Cruise intervals (CI): Run at 10-K race pace to promote stamina and the ability to run strong when tired. For 10:00 goal pace (2:11:06), run 7:07 (1,200 m/1,312 yd), 4:45 (800 m/875 yd); for 9:00 pace (1:57:59), run 6:24 (1,200 m/1,312 yd), 4:16 (800 m/875 yd); for 8:00 pace (1:44:52), run 5:42 (1,200 m/1,312 yd), 3:48 (800 m/875 yd).

Pace intervals (PI): Relatively lengthy repetitions at your goal race pace to build endurance and develop pace judgment. Numbers in square brackets denote distance of recovery jog.

Mi: distance in miles

Rest: No running at all. You can walk, cycle, or swim if you do it casually.

Speed intervals (SI): Run at 5-K race pace to promote relaxed speed and a sense of comfort at your considerably slower half-marathon pace. For 10:00 goal pace, run 4:30 (800 m/875 yd), 2:15 (400 m/437 yd), 1:07 (200 m/219 yd); for 9:00 half-marathon pace, run 4:04 (800 m/875 yd), 2:02 (400 m/437 yd), 1:01 (200 m/219 yd); for 8:00 half-marathon pace, run 3:37 (800 m/875 yd), 1:48 (400 m/437 yd), 0:54 (200 m/219 yd).

Strides (S): Over 100 m (109 yd), gradually accelerate to 90% of all-out, hold it for 5 seconds, then decelerate. Walk to full recovery after each.

Total uphill time (TUT): Work the uphill sections during your run, at something near a strong 10-K effort in the total time called for.

and may even have finished a half-marathon. Now you have a specific finishing time in mind, and will train hard to achieve it.

You'll need increased weekly distance plus an adequate long run, as well as some faster runs.

You'll also do some interval runs at faster times than your projected race pace.

On race day, to warm up, jog just 800 m (875 yd), then do a few fast strides. Divide your half like this: 10-mile (16 km) run,

THE HALF-MARATHON RACE PLAN – ADVANCED								
WEEK	M	T	W	T	F	S	S	TOTAL
1	Rest	4x1-mi (1.6 km) PI [400 m/437 yd], 6x200 m (219 yd) SI [100 m/109 yd]	4 mi (6.4 km), or Rest	3 mi (4.8 km) PI, 2x800 m (875 yd) CI [200 m/219 yd] + 4x100 m (109 yd) S	4 mi (6.4 km), or Rest	6 mi (9.6 km) + 4x100 m (109 yd) S	13 mi (20.9 km) LR	40–45 mi (64.3–72.4 km)
2	Rest	4x1-mi (1.6 km) PI [400 m/437 yd], 6x200 m (219 yd) SI [100 m/109 yd]	4 mi (6.4 km), or Rest	3 mi (4.8 km) PI, 2x800 m (875 yd) CI [200 m/219 yd] + 4x100 m (109 yd) S	4 mi (6.4 km), or Rest	6 mi (9.6 km) + 4x100 m (109 yd) S	14 mi (22.5 km) LRFF	40–45 mi (64.3–72.4 km)
3	Rest	FFI 2x(400 m [437 yd] SI {100 m/109 yd}, 1,200 m [1,312 yd] CI {200 m/219 yd}, 2000 m [2,187 yd] PI)	4 mi (6.4 km) + 6x100 fast strides	4 mi (6.4 km) PI	Rest	5-K race	10 mi (16.1 km) LR	35 mi (56.3 km)
4	Rest	3x1.5-mi (2.4 km) CI [400 m/437 yd]	4 mi (6.4 km), or Rest	6 mi (9.6 km) alternating 2:00–3:00 CI w/1:00 jogs	3 mi (4.8 km) easy, or Rest	6 mi (9.6 km) + 6x100 m (109 yd) S	15 mi (24.1 km) LRS	42–47 mi (67.5–75.6 km)
5	Rest	FFI 2x(400 m [437 yd] SI {100 m/109 yd}, 1,200 m [1,312 yd] CI {200 m/219 yd}, 2400 m [2,624 yd] PI)	4 mi (6.4 km), or Rest	6 mi (9.6 km) alternating 2:00–3:00 CI w/1:00 jogs	3 mi (4.8 km) easy, or Rest	6 mi (9.6 km) + 6x100 m (109 yd) S	16 mi (25.7 km) LRF	42–47 mi (67.5–75.6 km)
6	Rest	4x1, 200 m (219 yd) CI {200 m/219 yd}, 6x200 m (219 yd) SI {100 m/109 yd}	4 mi (6.4 km), or Rest	2x(400m [437 yd] SI {100 m/109 yd}, 800 m [875 yd] SI {200/19 yd}, 400 m [437 yd] SI)	Rest	10-K race	12 mi (19.3 km) LR	38 mi (61.1 km)

5-K race. Start running just slower than goal pace, then work into a rhythm and run just below your lactate threshold level. Draft off other runners to conserve energy.

ADVANCED

You've run and raced for many years. You've entered, competed in, and finished just about every distance – half-marathon and maybe even a full marathon – and have averaged 35-plus miles (56 km) a week for at least the last six or seven months. You've run some personal records (PRs) at some shorter distances, and now you want to push yourself. And you're ready to step up and do more intense speedwork.

THE HALF-MARATHON RACE PLAN – ADVANCED

WEEK	M	T	W	T	F	S	S	TOTAL
7	Rest	FFI 2x(400 m [437 yd] SI {100 m/109 yd}, 1,200 m [1,312 yd] CI {200 m/219 yd}, 3,200 [3,499 yd] PI)	3 mi (4.8 km) PI	5–6 mi (8–9.6 km) PI	Rest	6 mi (9.6 km) + 6x100 m (109 yd) S	17 mi (27.3 km) LRS	44–50 mi (70.8–80.4 km)
8	Rest	2x1,200 m (219 yd) SI {400 m/437 yd}, 6x200 m (219 yd) SI {55 m/60 yd}, 2x1,200 m (1,312 yd) SI {400 m/437 yd}	3 mi (4.8 km) PI	6–7 mi (9.6–11 km) PI	Rest	6 mi (9.6 km) + 6x100 m (109 yd) fast S	10 mi (16.1 km) LR	44–50 mi (70.8–80.4 km)
9	Rest	6x400 (437 yd) CI {100 m/109 yd}	3 mi (4.8 km) PI	2x400 m (437 yd) CI {200 m/219 yd}, 2x200 m(219 yd) SI {100 m/109 yd}	Rest	3 mi (4.8 km) easy	Half-marathon race	

Cruise intervals (CI): Run at 10-K race pace to promote stamina and the ability to run strong when tired. For 8:00 goal pace (1:44:52), run 5:42 (1,200 m/1,312 yd), 3:48 (800 m/875 yd); for 7:00 pace (1:31:46), run 6:40 for 1.6 km (1 mile), 5:00 (1,200 m/1,312 yd), 3:20 (800 m/875 yd); for 6:00 pace (1:18:39), run 5:34 for 1.6 km (1 mile), 4:10 (1,200 m/1,312 yd), 2:47 (800 m/875 yd).

Fatigue fighter intervals (FFI): These intervals combine speed and pace intervals back-to-back (with very short recoveries) to work on maintaining pace and staying relaxed as you tire. Jog 5 to 7 minutes easy between sets.

Long run (LR): This means a moderate pace (roughly 60 to 75 seconds slower than your half-marathon goal pace).

Long run fartlek (LRF): Alternate one minute at 10-K pace with one-minute jogs in the middle third of the run.

Long run fast finish (LRFF): Run the final 15 minutes at 10-K pace.

Long run stamina (LRS): Run 4.6–9.6 km (3–6 miles) at half-marathon goal pace in the middle third of the run.

Pace intervals (PI): Relatively lengthy repetitions at your goal half-marathon per-mile/km pace to build endurance and develop pace judgment. Note: All numbers in curly brackets denote distance of recovery jog.

Mi: distance in miles

Rest: No running at all. You can walk, cycle, or swim if you do it casually.

Speed intervals (SI): Run at 5-K race pace to promote relaxed speed and a sense of comfort at your considerably slower half-marathon pace. If your half-marathon goal pace is 8:00 per mile (1:44:52), run 3:37 (800 m/875 yd), 1:48 (400 m/437 yd), 0:54 (200 m/ 219 yd); for 7:00 half-marathon pace, run 3:09 (800 m/875 yd), 1:35 (400 m/437 yd), 0:48 (200 m/219 yd); for 6:00 half pace, run 2:42 (800 m/875 yd), 1:22 (400 m/437 yd), 0:41 (200 m/219 yd).

Strides (S): Over 100 m (109 yd), gradually accelerate to 90% of all-out; hold it for 5 seconds, then decelerate. Walk to full recovery after each.

In this plan you'll be putting in some long runs and increasing your weekly distance. You'll also do some runs at half-marathon pace so your body will know what it feels like, and will do some short, subrace-pace repetitions followed by an extended run at your half-marathon goal speed to simulate the demands of the race.

Remember, on rest days you really don't want to be doing any running at all. Your body needs some down time to recover. If you are one of those people who just isn't comfortable taking a day off we recommend you do some light cross training activities. Otherwise, this programme should provide you with enough of a challenge.

Ultimate Marathon Plan

The marathon has a cachet all its own, and is a dream of many runners. If you're ready to commit the time and effort, you can be ready in just 16 weeks.

Short races (5-K to 10-K) are great fitness boosters that let you run much faster than your marathon goal pace – an effort you can't replicate in training, no matter how motivated you are. So all these training schedules feature two races to help boost aerobic capacity and lactate threshold.

All of your non-race training weeks will be repeated – weeks one and two, for example, will be the same. This lets you make adaptations in pace and recovery based on your experience, and gives you an opportunity to master one cycle before moving on to the next, more rigorous one.

In training, run on even grass or hard-packed dirt whenever possible to reduce impact.

BEGINNER

You've run 15–20 miles (24–32 km) a week for at least six months, completed a 5-K or 10-K, or something longer. You can run 5–6 miles (8–10 km) easily and want to

become a stronger overall runner able to finish your first marathon. Your actual finishing time is not really your top concern.

You're going to run three to four days a week and gradually increase your weekly distance to 35 miles (56 km) or more a week. You will do a weekend long run, and also include some hill running and aerobic intervals.

You're also going to run two low-key races to get the feel of competition. Many runners choose a half-marathon as part of their pre-marathon training.

On race day, make a conscious effort to run slower than you feel like you should for the first 12–13 miles (19–21 km). It's easy to get caught up in the excitement and run faster times than you're accustomed to. You don't want to burn yourself out. Look around, chat with those around you. Walk through the aid stations, drink fluids, take a break, then slowly resume your running.

Running a marathon is an experience of a lifetime that takes a firm commitment and months of training.

THE MARATHON RACE PLAN – BEGINNERS

WEEK	M	T	W	T	F	S	S	TOTAL
1	Rest	4 mi (6.4 km), including 4:00 TUT	Rest	1-hour run	Rest	4 mi (6.4 km)	6 mi (9.6 km)	15–16 mi (24–25.7 km)
2	Rest	4 mi (6.4 km), including 4:00 TUT	Rest	1-hour run	Rest	4 mi (6.4 km)	7 mi (11.2 km)	15–16 mi (24–25.7 km)
3	Rest	4 mi (6.4 km), including 5:00 TUT	Rest	6 mi (9.6 km)	Rest	Rest	8 mi (12.8 km)	18–19 mi (29–30.5 km)
4	Rest	4 mi (6.4 km), including 5:00 TUT	Rest	6 mi (9.6 km)	Rest	Rest	9 mi (14.4 km)	18–19 mi (29–30.5 km)
5	Rest	4 mi (6.4 km), including 3x2:00 AI	Rest	4 mi (6.4 km)	Rest	5K race	6–8 mi (9.6–12.8 km)	19–21 mi (30.5–33.8 km)
6	Rest	5 mi (8 km), including 6:00 TUT	Rest	7 mi (11.2 km)	Rest	Rest	10 mi (16.1 km)	22–24 mi (35.4–38.6 km)
7	Rest	5 mi (8 km), including 6:00 TUT	Rest	7 mi (11.2 km)	Rest	Rest	12 mi (19.3 km)	22–24 mi (35.4–38.6 km)
8	Rest	5 mi (8 km), including 7:00 TUT	Rest	8 mi (12.8 km)	Rest	Rest	12 mi (19.3 km)	25–27 mi (40.2–43.4 km)
9	Rest	5 mi (8 km), including 7:00 TUT	Rest	8 mi (12.8 km)	Rest	Rest	14 mi (22.5 km)	25–27 mi (40.2–43.4 km)
10	Rest	5 mi (8 km), including 3x3:00 AI	Rest	4 mi (6.4 km)	Rest	10K race	5 mi (8 km)	24 mi (38.6 km)
11	Rest	5 mi (8 km), including 8:00 TUT	Rest	9 mi (14.4 km)	Rest	Rest	16 mi (25.7 km)	30–32 mi (48.2–51.5 km)
12	Rest	5 mi (8 km), including 8:00 TUT	Rest	9 mi (14.4 km)	Rest	Rest	18 mi (28.9 km)	30–32 mi (48.2–51.5 km)
13	Rest	5 mi (8 km), including 9:00 TUT	Rest	10 mi (16.1 km)	Rest	4 mi (6.4 km)	20 mi (32.2 km)	39 mi (62.7 km)
14	Rest	5 mi (8 km), including 9:00 TUT	Rest	10 mi (16.1 km)	Rest	4 mi (6.4 km)	10 mi (16.1 km)	29 mi (46.6 km)
15	Rest	3 mi (4.8 km), including 3X3:00 AI	Rest	5 mi (8 km)	Rest	3 mi (4.8 km), including 3x2:00 AI	5 mi (8 km)	16 mi (25.7 km)
16	Rest	3 mi (4.8 km), Including 3x2:00 AI	Rest	3 mi (4.8 km) jog	Rest	2 mi (3.2 km) jog	Marathon	

Aerobic intervals (AI): Timed repetitions of 2–3 minutes slightly faster than your normal training pace – enough to make you breathe harder, but not go anaerobic (panting, gasping, verge-of-out-of-breath). Jog slowly after each repetition until you are refreshed enough to run the next.

Mi: distance in miles

Rest: No running at all. You can walk, cycle, or swim if you do it casually.

Total uphill time (TUT): The total number of minutes you spend running semi-vigorously up inclines.

INTERMEDIATE

You have been running 20–30 miles (32–48 km) a week for a year or more. You do a weekly long run of 8–10 miles (13–16 km) and have some experience with tempo runs or intervals. You've run 10-K races, probably finished a half-marathon, maybe even a full marathon. But now you have a specific goal time in mind.

What's in store? Long runs with higher-level running twice weekly, including sustained tempo runs at your half-marathon race pace. You are also going to be doing a little speedwork.

Before each Tuesday and Thursday session, run 15 minutes easy, followed by 4x100 m (109 yd) strides, and run 15 minutes easy at the end.

On race day, go 10–15 seconds per mile slower than your goal pace for the first 5–8 miles (8–13 km) – for a big payoff later. Then at 18–20 miles (29–32 km), you'll have some gas in the tank.

There is no guarantee that you won't still hit a wall at mile 21 or so. If this happens, and your legs suddenly get heavy, rely on your mental strength to carry you through. You can do this.

AVOID CHAFING

We know you want to avoid those painful little patches of raw skin that can appear after a few miles of running (and rubbing). Problem spots are the nipples, along bra lines, under the arms, and between the thighs. Some solutions:

- Choose longer shorts or half-leg tights that hug your legs.
- Choose high-tech synthetic fabrics that wick moisture away from your skin. Avoid cotton.
- Race in broken-in clothing; avoid new or untested clothing.
- Wear your running bra inside out to keep seams away from your skin.
- Slather lubricant such as petroleum jelly on vulnerable areas such as feet, inner thighs, and nipples. At a pinch, even lip balm will help.
- Try cushioning products for friction-prone areas; these peel off easily after your run.

WEEK	M	T	W	T	F	S	S	TOTAL
				THE MARATHON RACE PLAN – INTERMEDIATE				
1	Rest	2 mi (3.2 km) GP, 2 mi (3.2 km) T, 2 mi (3.2 km) GP	3 mi (4.8 km), 4x100 m (109 yd) S	1-hour run, including 4:00–5:00 TUT	Rest	4 mi (6.4 km)	8 mi (12.8 km)	29–33 mi (46.6–53.1 km)
2	Rest	2 mi (3.2 km) GP, 2 mi (3.2 km) T, 2 mi (3.2 km) GP	3 mi (4.8 km), 4x100 m (109 yd) S	1-hour run, including 4:00–5:00 TUT	Rest	4 mi (6.4 km)	10 mi (16.1 km)	29–33 mi (46.6–53.1 km)
3	Rest	2 mi (3.2 km) GP, 4x1 mi (1.6 km) T, (1:00) 2 mi (3.2 km) GP	3 mi (4.8 km), 5x100 m (109 yd) S	70-minute run, including 5:00–6:00 TUT	Rest	5 mi (8 km)	12 mi (19.3 km)	35–39 mi (56.3–62.7 km)
4	Rest	2 mi (3.2 km) GP, 4x1 mi (1.6 km) T, (1:00) 2 mi (3.2 km) GP	3 mi (4.8 km), 5x100 m (109 yd) S	70-minute run, including 5:00–6:00 TUT	Rest	5 mi (8 km)	14 mi (22.5 km)	35–39 mi (56.3–62.7 km)
5	Rest	4x1,200 m (1,312 yd) C	3 mi (4.8 km), 4x100 m (109 yd) S	4x800 m (875 yd) SI	Rest	5K race	10 mi (16.1 km)	28–30 mi (45–48.2 km)
6	Rest	2 mi (3.2 km) GP, 2x2 mi (3.2 km)T, 3 mi (4.8 km) GP	3 mi (4.8 km), 6x100 m (109 yd) S	80-minute run, including 6:00–8:00 TUT	Rest	5 mi (8 km)	15 mi (24.1 km)	39–43 mi (62.7–69.1 km)
7	Rest	2 mi (3.2 km) GP, 2x2 mi T, 3 mi (4.8 km) GP	3 mi (4.8 km), 6x100 m (109 yd) S	80-minute run, including 6:00–8:00 TUT	Rest	5 mi (8 km)	16 mi (25.7 km)	39–43 mi (62.7–69.1 km)
8	Rest	2 mi (3.2 km) GP, 3x2 mi (3.2 km) T, (2:00) 3 mi (4.8 km) GP	3 mi (4.8 km), 6x100 m (109 yd) S	4x1 mi (1.6 km)	Rest	5 mi (8 km)	16 mi (25.7 km)	44–47 mi (70.8–75.6 km)
9	Rest	2 mi (3.2 km) GP, 3x2 mi (3.2 km) T, (2:00) 3 mi (4.8 km) GP	3 mi (4.8 km), 6x100 m (109 yd) S	4x1 mi (1.6 km)	Rest	5 mi (8 km)	17 mi (27.3 km)	44–47 mi (70.8–75.6 km)
10	Rest	1-hour run, including 2x1,200 m (1,312 yd) CI, 2x400 m (437 yd) SI	4 mi (6.4 km)	4x800 m (875 yd) S, 6x100 (109 yd) S	Rest	10K race	6–8 mi (9.6–12.8 km)	32–34 mi (51.5–54.7 km)
11	Rest	2 mi (3.2 km) GP, 4x2 mi (3.2 km) T, (2:00) 3 mi (4.8 km) GP	3 mi (4.8 km), 6x100 m (109 yd) S	90-minute run, including 8:00–10:00 TUT	Rest	4 mi (6.4 km)	18 mi (28.9 km)	45–51 mi (72.4–82 km)

THE MARATHON RACE PLAN – INTERMEDIATE

WEEK	M	T	W	T	F	S	S	TOTAL
12	Rest	2 mi (3.2 km) GP, 4x2 mi (3.2 km) T, (2:00) 3 mi (4.8 km) GP	3 mi (4.8 km) 6x100 m (109 yd) S	90-minute run, including 8:00–10:00 TUT	Rest	4 mi (6.4 km)	19 mi (30.5 km)	45–51 mi (72.4–82 km)
13	Rest	3x1 mi (1.6 km) C, 3x800 m (875 yd) SI	3 mi (4.8 km), 6x100 m (109 yd) S	75-minute run, including 6:00–8:00 TUT	Rest	4 mi (6.4 km)	20 mi (32.3 km)	46 mi (74 km)
14	Rest	3x1 mi (1.6 km) CI, 3x 800 m (875 yd) SI	3 mi (4.8 km), 6x100 m (109 yd) S	75-minute run, including 6:00–8:00 TUT	Rest	4 mi (6.4 km)	13 mi (20.9 km)	45 mi (72.4 km)
15	Rest	2 mi (3.2 km) GP, 4 mi (6.4 km) T	3 mi (4.8 km), 6x100 m (109 yd) S	1-hour run, including 6x400 m (437 yd) SI	Rest	Rest	1-hour run	27–29 mi (43.4–46.6 km)
16	Rest	4x400 m (437 yd) SI	Rest	3 mi (4.8 km) 6x100 m (109 yd) S	Rest	2-mi (3.2 km) jog	Marathon	

Cruise intervals (CI): For 11:00 goal pace, run 9:56 (1 mile/1.6 km), 7:49 (1,312 yd/1,200 m); for 10:00 pace, run 9:02 and 6:47; for 9:00 pace, run 8:07 and 6:06. Recovery is half the distance of the repetition.
Goal pace (GP): Your per-mile goal marathon pace.
Mi: distance in miles
Rest: No running at all. You can walk, cycle, or swim if you do it casually.
Strides (S): Gradual, smooth accelerations over 100 m (109 yd) (straight section on a track), running fast and controlled over the middle third – but never sprinting – then gradually decelerating. Walk to full recovery after each.
Speed intervals (SI): For 11:00 pace, run 4:52 (800 m/875 yd), 2:26 (400 m/437 yd); for 10:00 pace, run 4:17, 2:08; for 9:00 pace, run 3:50, 1:55. Recovery is equal distance (for example, 400 m/437 yd jog for 400 m/437 yd repeats). Run 15 minutes easy followed by 4x100 m (109 yd) strides before each session and 15 minutes easy at the end.
Tempo runs (T): For 11:00 goal pace (4:48:25), run 10:28 (1 mile/1.6 km); for 10:00 pace (4:22:12), run 9:31; for 9:00 pace (3:55:58), run 8:34. Recovery is slow jogging for the number of minutes in parentheses.
Total uphill time (TUT): The total number of minutes you spend running semi-vigorously up inclines, either repeats up the same hill or total uphill time over a hilly loop.

ADVANCED

You've been running three or four years and log 35–40 miles (56–64 km) a week. You've raced all distances and now want to score the absolute fastest 26.2 miles you can.

You're going to need to run as much as 50 miles (80 km) a week. Along with long runs, you'll spend two days a week developing stamina at half-marathon, 10-K, and 5-K race pace. On Thursdays, you'll do a marathon goal pace/tempo/cruise combo – an extended effort that develops strength. Before Tuesday and Thursday sessions, run 15 minutes easy, then 4x100 m (109 yd) strides, and 15 minutes easy at the end. On race day, run the first mile 15–20 seconds slower than usual pace.

								THE MARATHON RACE PLAN – ADVANCED
WEEK	M	T	W	T	F	S	S	TOTAL
1	Rest	4x1 mi (1.6 km) CI	4 mi (6.4 km), 4x100 m (109 yd) S	2 mi (3.2 km) GP, 2–3 mi (3.2–4,8 km) T, 2 mi (3.2 km) GP	Rest	45–60 minutes easy	10 mi (16.1km) WH	34–40 mi (54.7–64.3 km)
2	Rest	4x1 mi (1.6 km) CI	4 mi (6.4 km), 4x100 m (109 yd) S	2 mi (3.2 km) GP, 2–3 mi (3.2–4,8 km) T, 2 mi (3.2 km) GP	Rest	45–60 minutes easy	11 mi (17.7 km) FF	34–40mi (54.7–64.3 km)
3	Rest	8–10 mi (12.8–16.1 km), including 6:00 TUT	4 mi (6.4 km), 6x100 m (109 yd) S	2 mi (3.2 km) GP, 4 mi (6.4 km) T, 2 mi (3.2 km) GP	Rest	45–60 minutes easy	12 mi (19.3 km)	38–44 mi (61.1–70.8 km)
4	Rest	8–10 mi (12.8–16.1 km), including 6:00 TUT	4 mi (6.4 km), 6x100 m (109 yd) S	2 mi (3.2 km) GP, 4 mi (6.4 km) T, 2 mi (3.2 km) GP	Rest	45–60 minutes easy	13 mi (21 km) FF	38–44 mi (61.1–70.8 km)
5	Rest	2x3 mi (4.8 km)T	4 mi (6.4 km), 6x100 m (109 yd) S	4x800 m (875 yd) SI, 4x400 m (437 yd) SI	Rest	5K race	12 mi (19.3 km)	34-36 mi (54.7–57.9 km)
6	Rest	10 mi (16.1 km), including 8:00 TUT	4 mi (6.4 km), 6x100 m (109 yd) S	3 mi (4.8 km) GP, 3–4x800 m (875 yd) CI, 3 mi (4.8 km) T	Rest	45–60 minute easy	14 mi (22.5 km)	40–50 mi (64.3–80.4 km)
7	Rest	10 mi (16.1 km), including 8:00 TUT	4 mi (6.4 km) 6x100 m (109 yd) S	3 mi (4.8 km)GP, 3–4x800 m (875 yd) CI, 3 mi (4.8 km) T	Rest	45–60 minutes easy	16 mi (25.7 km) FF	40–50 mi (64.3–80.4 km)
8	Rest	2x1 mi (1.6 km) CI, 4x800 (875 yd) SI, 2x1 mi (1.6 km) CI	4 mi (6.4 km), 6x100 m (109 yd) S	3 mi (4.8 km) GP, 4–6x800 m (875 yd) CI, 3 mi T (4.8 km)	Rest	45–60 minutes easy	18 mi (28.9 km)	47–53 mi (75.6–85.3 km)
9	Rest	2x1 mi (1.6 km) CI, 4x800 m (875 yd) SI, 2x1 mi (1.6 km) CI	4 mi (6.4 km), 6x100 m (109 yd) S	3 mi (4.8 km) GP, 4–6x800 m (875 yd) CI, 3 mi (4.8 km)T	Rest	45–60 minutes easy	20 mi (32.2 km)	47–53 mi (75.6–85.3 km)
10	Rest	2x4 mi (6.4 km) T	4 mi (6.4 km), 6x100 m (109 yd) S	4x800 m (875 yd) SI, 4x400 m (437 yd) SI	Rest	10K race	10 mi (16.1 km)	34–36 mi (54.7–57.9 km)
11	Rest	10–12 mi (16.1–19.3 km), including 10:00 TUT	4 mi (6.4 km), 6x100 m (109 yd) S	3 mi (4.8 km) GP, 6–8x800 m (875 yd) CI, 3 mi (4.8 km) T	Rest	45–60 minutes easy	20 mi (32.2 km) FF	51–55 mi (82–88.5 km)
12	Rest	10–12 mi (16.1–19.3 km), including 10:00 TUT	4 mi (6.4 km), 6x100 m (109 yd) S	3 mi (4.8 km) GP, 6–8x800 m (875 yd) CI, 3 mi (4.8 km) T	Rest	45–60 minutes easy	22 mi (35.4 km)	53–57 mi (85.3–91.7 km)

THE MARATHON RACE PLAN – ADVANCED								
WEEK	M	T	W	T	F	S	S	TOTAL
13	Rest	8–10 mi (12.8–16.1 km), including 6:00 TUT	4 mi (6.4 km), 6x100 m (109 yd) S	4x1 mi (1.6 km) CI, 2x800 m (875 yd) SI	Rest	45–60 minutes easy	20 mi (32.1 km) WH	43–47 mi (69.2–75.6 km)
14	Rest	8–10 mi (12.8–16.1 km), including 6:00 TUT	4 mi (6.4 km), 6x100 m (109 yd) S	4x1 mi (1.6 km) CI, 2x800 m (875 yd) SI	Rest	45–60 minutes easy	13 mi (20.9 km) FF	36–40 mi (57.9–64.3 km)
15	Rest	4x400 m (437 yd) SI, 2x800 m (875 yd) CI, 4x400 m (437 yd) SI	4 mi (6.4 km), 6x100 m (109 yd) S	2 mi (3.2 km), 2x800 m (875 yd) CI, 2x400 m (437 yd) SI	Rest	5 mi (8 km)	60–75-minute run	34–37 mi (54.7–59.5 km)
16 Taper	Rest	2 mi (3.2 km) T, 2x800 m (875 yd) C, 2x400 m (437 yd) SI	3 mi easy, 4x100 m (109 yd) S	4x400 m (437 yd) SI	Rest	3 mi (4.8 km) jog	Marathon	

Cruise intervals (CI): For 8:00 goal pace, run 7:14 (1 mile/1.6 km), 3:37 (875 yd/800 m); for 7:00 pace, run 6:19 and 3:09; for 6:00 pace, run 5:25 and 2:43. Recovery is 2–3 minutes for mile repeats, 1–2 for 800 m (875 yd).
FF: fast finish; do tempo pace for the final 15 minutes of the run.
Goal pace (GP): Your per-mile marathon goal pace.
Mi: distance in miles
Strides (S): Gradual, smooth accelerations over 100 m (109 yd), running fast and controlled over the middle third – but never sprinting – then just as gradually decelerating. Walk to full recovery after each.
Speed intervals (SI): For 8:00 goal pace, run 3:27 (800 m/875 yd), 1:42 (400 m/437 yd); for 7:00 pace, run 2:59 and 1:30; for 6:00 pace, do 2:36 and 1:18. Recovery is 2–3 minutes for 800 m (875 yd) repeats, 1–2 minutes for 400 m (437 yd).
Tempo runs (T): For 8:00 goal pace, run 7:38 (1 mile/1.6 km); for 7:00 pace (3:03:32), run 6:39; for 6:00 pace (2:37:19), run 5:43.
Total uphill time (TUT): The total number of minutes you spend running semi-vigorously up inclines, either repeats up the same hill or total uphill time over a hilly loop.
WH: with hills; do part of the run over a hilly or undulating course.

Track training can be monotonous but it's much easier to figure how much distance you've put in.

The Perfect Form

Paying close attention to your running form is every bit as important as what type of shoes you wear. You might be in top physical shape but if you run with your arms flailing all over the place you're needlessly wasting energy. Having perfect form makes for efficient running. Here are some tips that will help make you a more effective runner.

Correct running posture will help you avoid injury and make you a more efficient runner.

Head tilt How you hold your head is the key component to your overall posture, which in turn determines how efficiently you run. Look ahead naturally, not down at your feet, and scan the horizon. This will straighten your neck and back, and bring them into alignment. Don't allow your chin to jut out. Just keep your head upright and try to stay relaxed.

Shoulders Shoulders help keep your upper body relaxed, which is critical to maintaining efficient running posture. Keep your shoulders low and loose, not high and tight. As you tire, don't let your shoulders creep up. If they do, shake them out to release the tension. Your shoulders also need to remain level and not dip from side to side with each stride.

Arms Your hands control the tension in your upper body, while your arm swing works in conjunction with your leg stride to drive you forward. Keep your hands in an unclenched fist, with your fingers lightly touching your palms. Your arms should swing mostly forward and back, not across your body, between waist and lower-chest level. Your elbows should be bent at about a 90-degree angle. When you feel your fists clenching or your forearms tensing, drop your arms to your sides and shake them out to release the tension.

Torso The position of your head and shoulders affects the position of your torso. With your head up and looking ahead and your shoulders low and loose, your torso and back naturally straighten to allow you to run in an efficient, upright position that promotes optimal lung capacity and stride length. Stretch yourself up to your full height with your back comfortably straight. If you start to slouch, take a deep breath and feel yourself straighten naturally. As you exhale simply maintain that upright position.

Hips Your hips are your centre of gravity, and key to good running posture. With your torso and back comfortably upright and straight, your hips naturally fall into proper alignment, pointing you straight ahead. If you allow your torso to hunch over or lean too far forward, your pelvis will tilt forward as well, which can put pressure on your lower back and throw the rest of your lower body out of alignment.

Legs and stride Efficient endurance running requires just a slight knee lift, a quick leg turnover, and a short stride. Together, these will facilitate fluid forward movement instead of diverting energy. Your feet should land directly under your body, and as your foot strikes the ground, your knee should be slightly flexed so that it bends naturally on impact. If your lower leg extends out in front of your body, your stride is too long. Overstriding can lead to injury.

Ankles and feet To run well, you need to push off the ground with maximum force. With each step, your foot should hit the ground lightly, landing between your heel and midfoot, then quickly roll forward. Keep your ankle flexed as your foot rolls forward to create more force for push-off. As you roll onto your toes, try to spring off the ground. You should feel your calf muscles propelling you forward on each step.

SPEED TRAINING ON GRASS

Why run on grass when a track offers stable footing and an accurate measure of distance? Exactly.

The hard surface of a paved trail or a track, coupled with the sure footing, give you an effective push-off with every stride. But much of the energy you exert when you run on grass goes into the earth instead of rebounding back into your feet and lower legs. So when you run on grass your cardiovascular system works harder than it does when you run on a track. Yes, intervals run on grass will be slower than those run on a track. But you'll get stronger from running an occasional workout on grass, as you force your body to work harder to overcome the slower surface.

Because grass surfaces are more unstable than a track, you'll work your stabilizer muscles, such as the internal and external obliques in your torso. The softer surface of grass also means less stress on your feet and lower legs, which can reduce your risk of stress fractures or shinsplints.

And moving your workout from the track to grass can take away the pressure you might feel to hit specific times for specific distances. Instead, run hard for a predetermined amount of time rather than for a given distance.

Running Glossary

Running comes with its own set of unique terminology that can often sound like a foreign language. Don't worry, it's not as difficult as all that. Here is a rundown of some familiar running terms and what they mean.

Anaerobic Threshold (AT)
The point at which you begin working your muscles without oxygen; above this point your blood lactate levels skyrocket – a gulping-and-gasping prelude to your engine shutting down.

Bandit
A runner who runs in an event without being registered. Sounds nefarious, but once upon a time that was the only way certain groups of people could get into races. Back when marathons wouldn't allow women or men over 40 to participate, running as a bandit was the only way those runners could compete. (We strongly suggest you follow standard registration procedures.)

Carbo-loading
Loading up on carbohydrates, such as pasta, bread, and rice. By increasing your intake of carbohydrates before the race, you'll have more muscle fuel available and will increase your endurance.

Try getting three-quarters of your food in the form of carbohydrates the four days before your race, particularly the day before. The idea is to avoid running out of sugar.

Cool-down
A period of slow running, jogging or walking after a run to help relax the muscles and aid in ridding them of lactic acid build-up.

CR (Course Record)
The best time run on a particular course.

Crashing and burning
In simple terms, this is what happens when you run out of fuel, and suddenly feel like you're running in quicksand. Because your body has run out of available sugar, it has started burning a higher ratio of fat – a process which, because it must first convert fats to sugars, entails some 20 metabolic steps compared with the 10 or so for burning glucose. This takes extra time and slows you down.

DNF (Did Not Finish)
A designation given to runners who are unable to finish a race. If you drop out at mile 16 of a marathon, a DNF will appear next to your name in the results listings.

DOMS (Delayed Onset Muscle Soreness)
Usually occurs around 48 hours after a long or intense run. You may feel fine the day after a long run, but it can take up to two days for the lactic acid to settle into your muscles. No matter how advanced your training regimen you can still experience DOMS.

Easy run
Just what it sounds like – running

Part of your evolution into a competitive runner will include learning some of the lingo.

at a comfortable pace so that you can maintain a conversation, without gasping for breath. Easy runs build aerobic fitness and muscular and skeletal strength, and prepare you for harder workouts. Should be 80 to 90% of your weekly distance.

Fartlek
Swedish for 'speed play'. Best done on grass or trails, you mix surges of hard running with easy running. Run fast bursts between phone boxes, lampposts or trees when you feel like it, and as hard an effort as you like.

Fun run
Often it's a community event with few or no prizes, and sometimes with a walking category. You'll have timers and sometimes plenty of support, such as volunteers at food and water stations, but the idea is to have fun.

Hill workout
Running up a hill at 85–90% effort, and jogging back down. This is a type of interval.

Intervals
Short periods of hard running followed by recovery periods, sometimes called VO2 max runs (see **VO2 Max**). Not only

Even during easy runs you should always pay attention to your form and stride length.

improves speed, but lets you work on your running form. Concentrate on arm and hand motion, posture, and stride length.

Junk distance
Runs done at a relaxed pace in order to meet a weekly or monthly distance quota. The term 'junk' is something of a misnomer as these easy runs can really help you recover from harder workouts and should be part of your training.

If you're looking to liven up the same old route, insert some pick-ups or fatleks into your next run.

Lactate Threshold (LT)

The point at which your muscles produce too much lactic acid, which breaks down into products that change your pH and decrease muscle efficiency (producing that burning sensation). When you train at LT pace (where your body produces more lactic acid), your body conditions itself to move lactate around. The build-up of lactic acid in your muscles causes muscle soreness (see **DOMS**).

Maximum heart rate

The highest heart rate reached during a specified period of time such as a minute. Your maximum heart rate is generally highest during childhood and steadily declines as you get older.

Negative splits

Running the second half of a race faster than the first half. Often considered to be a good physio-logical strategy, and it also works

Pick-ups

Short periods of acceleration during a run. These differ from fartleks in that they are more brief in time and distance, and are simply a way to break up the monotony of an easy run.

Running economy

This is a reference to the amount of oxygen you use when you run. As your economy improves, you are able to run using a smaller percentage of your maximum oxygen consumption capabilities (see **VO2 Max**).

Speedwork

Shorter than race distance repetitions at or below your goal race pace. Can be hard to very hard to nearly flat-out. Produces leg speed, elevated lactate threshold, stamina, biomechanical efficiency, and the ability to tolerate the discomfort that's essential to racing fitness.

psychologically as well. Keeping your early splits slower can save energy for your final kick.

Personal Record (PR)

Also PB (Personal Best). Just what it sounds like – your best time for a specific event or distance. Obviously, if you've never raced before, whatever your time is, it's going to be your PR. Keeping track of your time records is a great way to keep yourself motivated.

Tapering

The process of cutting back on your training distance anywhere from several days to several weeks (depending on the length of a race) before running a race. This gives muscles a chance to rest, recover, and be in top competitive shape on race day.

Tempo run
Running harder than your usual pace, either continuously or in intervals with short recoveries. Should be done at a comfortably hard pace.

VO2 Max The maximum amount of oxygen that a runner can extract from the atmosphere and transfer to the body's muscles and tissues.

The Wall
This is what you hit after you crash and burn. When you hit it, you'll know. Not a good thing. (See **Carbo-loading**.) Reach for a sports drink and easily digestible food. Ease your wobbly legs to the ground and breathe deeply. The best way to avoid the wall is a combination of physical and mental preparation. Make sure you train for the proper distance for your particular race, knowing in your mind that you have already run that same distance is half the battle.

When you hit the wall, get yourself some food and drink and keep your focus.

PART III:
COMPLEMENTING YOUR TRAINING

A Winning Diet

The fuel you put into your body can make a tremendous difference to your performance—and the fuel you need will vary according to your weekly distance. Here are three basic eating plans, designed for 5-K and 10-K runners, half-marathoners, and marathoners. The calories and food quantities are based on a 68–72.5 kg (150–160 lbs) runner. If you weigh less, you should eat the smaller quantities suggested. If you weigh more, eat more.

Lean meats and fresh fish are always welcome in competitive running nutrition plans.

5-K AND 10-K RACES

A 5-K or 10-K runner needs more calories, carbohydrate, and protein than an average person. A training run of 3.2–8 km (2–5 miles) burns an extra 200 to 500 calories, and running increases your protein needs by an additional 15 to 25 grams. You need the extra protein to rebuild muscle and produce new blood cells. For longer runs, include more carbohydrates on your long-run day which will help towards a faster recovery.

Before the race Eat a small meal before your race to top off your fuel tank and help you stay alert (especially if the start is early in the morning). Aim for 300 to 500 calories, two to four hours before the start. Your meal should be high in carbohydrate, and low in fat. Try an energy bar and 250 ml (8 fl. oz) of sports drink or a wholemeal bagel spread with jam, half a banana, and water.

During the race Because you're finishing your race within an hour, plain water is your best bet. Pause at least once during your 10-K to drink 120 ml (4 fl. oz) of fluid. (Drink more if it's hot.) Here's a sample meal plan:

Breakfast 227 g (8 oz) porridge with 200 ml (16 fl. oz) skimmed milk; one wholegrain English muffin spread with 2 tablespoons jam; one banana.

Morning snack 57 g (2 oz) trail mix (made with soy nuts, nuts, and raisins); 250 ml (8 fl. oz) green tea flavoured with 2 teaspoons honey.

Lunch One bean burrito made with one tortilla, 227 g (8 oz) black beans, 113 g (4 oz) rice, 28 g (1 oz) cheese, salsa; one sliced tomato; 227 g (8 oz) fresh fruit salad; two delicious oatmeal cookies

Snack One energy bar with a glass of water

Dinner 227 g (8 oz) pasta topped with 180 ml (6 fl. oz) marinara sauce, made with 85 g (3 oz) ground turkey or soy substitute; 454 g (16 oz) leafy green salad with 2 tablespoons reduced-fat dressing; two 28 g (1 oz) pieces of chocolate

HALF-MARATHON EATING PLAN

As a half-marathoner, you'll need more calories, carbohydrate, protein, and other nutrients than

	5-K AND 10-K	HALF-MARATHON	MARATHON
Weekly Distance	16–40 km (10–25 miles)	40.2–64.4 km (25–40 miles)	48.2–80.4 km (30–50 miles)
Calories	2,200 to 2,600	2,500 to 2,900	2,700 to 3,300
Carbohydrates	330–375 g (12–13 oz)	375–475 g (13–16.5 oz)	440–600 g (15.5–21 oz)
Protein	70–85 g (2.5–3 oz)	75–90 g (2.5–3 oz)	90–110 g (3–4 oz)
Fat	50–80 g (1.7–2.8 oz)	55–85 g (2.5–3 oz)	60–95 g (2 to 3.5 oz)

Leafy green vegetables are packed with vitamins and make a great pre- or post-meal snack.

people who run only 5-K and 10-K races. The extra carbohydrate will fuel your training, and the extra protein will help repair small muscle-fibre tears. As you bump up your distance, you'll need more healthy fats to help boost your immunity, especially omega-3 fats that are found in foods such as salmon and tuna.

Before the race Your 21-km (13.1-mile) effort will probably take anywhere from 75 minutes to more than two hours. You'll need to eat more before the race, as well as fuel up with carbohydrates during the run. Aim for 400 to 800 high-carbohydrate calories about three hours before the race. One possibility: two pancakes spread with three teaspoons jam, 250 ml (8 fl. oz) of sports drink, and half an energy bar.

During the race: You need to replenish fluids and calories. Aim for 150–200 ml (4–6 fl. oz) of water or sports drink every 15 to 20 minutes and about 100 calories every half-hour. Don't forget to count the calories in your sports drink as part of your carbohydrate intake (about 50 to 70 calories per 0.25 1/8 fl. oz). Fruit is another good high-carb choice.

Here's a sample meal plan:

Breakfast: Egg pitta (two scrambled eggs and 2 tablespoons salsa in a wholemeal pitta); 227 g (8 oz) fresh fruit salad; 250 ml (8 fl. oz) cranberry juice.

Morning snack: One small carton of low-fat yogurt with 1 tablespoon honey and 2 tablespoons chopped almonds.

Lunch: One salmon-salad sandwich. Two slices wholemeal bread, 57 g (2 oz) canned salmon with 2 teaspoons reduced fat mayo, 113 g (4 oz) chopped celery, one chopped dill pickle, and 57 g (2 oz) chopped corriander; one apple sliced and spread with 1 tablespoon peanut butter; two fig bars

Snack: Four dried pear halves; 500 ml (16 fl. oz) sports drink

Dinner: 85 g (3 oz) grilled chicken served over 227 g (8 oz) brown rice; 227 g (8 oz) steamed cauliflower and broccoli with 1 tablespoon grated Parmesan cheese; 113 g (4 oz) boiled red potatoes tossed with 57 g (2 oz) chopped parsley and 1 teaspoon olive oil; 150 ml (4 fl. oz) low-fat frozen yogurt topped with 227 g (8 oz) fresh strawberries and 2 tablespoons chocolate sauce.

MARATHON EATING PLAN

Training for a marathon seriously increases your nutritional needs. The extra distance boosts your calorie needs, and you'll need even more carbohydrate to recover from training runs. Studies show that you need to eat at least 3 to 5 grams of carbohydrate per 0.45 kg (1 lb) of body weight to fully restock your glycogen stores within 24 hours.

Eat plenty of wholesome foods rich in vitamins and minerals such as iron, zinc, and B vitamins. Taking a daily multivitamin/mineral supplement is also a good bit of nutritional insurance.

Whole grain cereals, porridge, and fresh fruit are smart choices for a race-day breakfast.

Flexibility Training

When it comes to runners, a seemingly innocuous subject such as stretching can spark arguments. There are those who believe that you should not stretch before a run but only after. Still others might debate that stretching prior to running is a crucial part of the warm-up. Rather than taking sides on this issue, we would like to offer that flexibility training is a beneficial component to any running regimen. Some light stretching before you run can help lengthen tight muscles and decrease your chances for pulls or tears. After you have finished your run, stretching will help rid your muscles of lactic acid, which causes soreness. The flexibility exercises featured here offer some basic runner's stretches with a 'twist' added to get more out of them.

Take time to incorporate stretching routines into your racing training plan.

HIP STRETCH

1 From a standing position, place your left foot on a bench and lean forward until you feel a stretch down the back of your right thigh.

2 Keep your right knee straight and rotate to the left side. Then slowly rotate to the right side.

3 Rotate from side to side for 30 to 60 seconds. Switch legs and repeat.

TRAINER'S TIP
Make sure to keep your back foot in contact with the floor and pointed forward at all times.

HAMSTRING STRETCH

1 Stand up straight with your legs shoulder width apart. Place your left foot on a bench and straighten your knee until you feel a stretch in your hamstring.

2 Lean forward slightly at the waist. Rotate to your right side and then back to your left.

3 Keeping your hands on your hips, rotate from side to side for 30 to 60 seconds. Switch legs and repeat.

CALF STRETCH

1 Stand with your right foot in front of your left. Place your hands against a wall. Lean forward and press your left heel down.

2 Curl the toes on your right foot and shift your weight to the outside of your left foot. Shift back and forth between this position and the starting position for 30 to 60 seconds. Switch legs and repeat.

DEEP CALF STRETCH

1 Stand with your left foot in front of your right. Place your hands against a wall. Shift more weight onto your left leg by bending your knee without lifting your heel.

2 Follow the same directions as Step 2 in the calf stretch (above) for 30 to 60 seconds. Switch legs and repeat.

Building Strength

Do you sometimes just not have enough strength at the end of a run or a race? Often a lack of upper body strength causes this slowdown. Keeping your arms pumping strongly will help drive your legs forward. Forceful breathing also helps your kick at the end of a run. To do this you need strong abdominal muscles. The following five exercises will help you run stronger across the finish line of any race. Do the weight exercises twice a week, completing one to three sets of 12 to 16 repetitions per set. Do the bicycle manoeuvre at least three times a week, doing one slow, controlled set of as many as you can do in good form.

SHOULDER SHRUG

TARGET: Upper trapezius muscles

1 Stand with your feet shoulder width apart. Hold one dumbbell in each hand with your hands down at your sides.

2 'Shrug' your shoulders up towards your ears, pause for a second, then slowly drop your shoulders back down. Repeat.

BENT-ARM LATERAL RAISE

TARGET: Deltoids

1 Hold one dumbbell in each hand with elbows in at your sides and arms bent at 90 degrees.

2 Keeping your back straight, slowly lift both elbows out and to shoulder level.

TRAINER'S TIP
Try to choose a weight that is about 65% of the maximum you can lift at any one time.

3 Slowly lower your elbows back down to your sides. Repeat.

STANDING BICEPS CURL
TARGET: Biceps

1 Stand with your legs shoulder width apart. Hold a dumbbell in each hand with your palms facing out and arms at your sides.

TRAINER'S TIP
When doing this exercise make sure you only lift with your forearms.

2 Keeping your back straight, slowly curl both forearms up to your shoulders.

3 Lower your forearms back down to your sides. Repeat.

TRICEPS CURL
TARGET: Triceps

1 Stand with both arms over your head and hold the end of one dumbbell between the fingers of both hands.

2 Keeping your elbows tucked in toward your ears, drop your forearms behind your head to shoulder level, then straighten them back up to the starting position.

BICYCLE MANOEUVRE
TARGET: Abdominals

1 Lie on your back with your hands behind your head, with your shoulders and upper back slightly off the ground. Extend both legs, keeping your feet about 15 cm (6 in) off the ground.

2 Alternate bringing in your opposite knee to meet your opposite elbow.

Springing into Action

Plyometrics (explosive jumping exercises) can significantly improve your running efficiency. In one study, running efficiency improved 8%, and 5-K times improved up to 30 seconds after just nine weeks of plyometrics. The theory is that plyometric training enhances your muscles' ability to generate power, making it easier to run harder. These simple drills teach the proprioceptors, sensory receptors which enable co-ordinated movement and balance, to push off the ground with greater force. For more spring in your step, make them a regular part of your workouts.

Plyometrics help develop fast-twitch muscles that can give you and extra burst when you need it.

SQUAT THRUST

1 Start from a standing position with your legs shoulder width apart.

2 Squat down and place your hands on the ground slightly in front of and beside your feet.

TRAINER'S TIP
Do these as quickly as you can while maintaining your form.

3 Thrust your legs out behind you into a push-up position. Then quickly pull your legs back under your body back into the squat and jump up. Do one to three sets of 12 to 15 repetitions each.

MOUNTAIN CLIMBERS

1 Stand on the ground and place your left foot on a 25–30.5 cm (10–12 in) high box.

2 Jump as high as you can and switch legs so that you land with the right foot on the box and your left foot on the ground.

3 Jump again so that your left foot lands on the box. Perform 10 to 15 repetitions. Do one to three sets.

TRAINER'S TIP
Remember that one repetition of this exercise equals a single jump off each foot.

LATERAL BOX JUMPS

1 Stand on the right side of a 10–15 cm (4–6 in) high box. Jump to the left side of the box.

2 Then quickly jump back again to the right side of the box. Try to keep your elbows tucked in.

3 Quickly reverse direction again, repeating back and forth for 30 to 60 seconds. Do one to three sets.

TRAINER'S TIP
To increase the degree of difficulty, you can raise the height of the box as you progress.

DOUBLE LEG JUMPS

1 Find an area with a lot of free space. Stand with your legs about shoulder-width apart.

TRAINER'S TIP
To get the most out of these jumps, swing your arms back and forth to help propel you forward.

2 Using both legs, bend your knees and jump forward as far as you can.

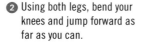

3 As soon as you touch the ground jump forward again. Do three jumps as a set and complete three to four sets.

STADIUM JUMPS

1 Stand at the base of stairs with you feet shoulder width apart and your hands behind your head.

2 Using both legs, bend your knees and jump one or two steps at a time, landing on the balls of your feet.

TRAINER'S TIP
As this exercise becomes easier you can increase the difficulty by doing it one leg at a time.

3 Perform a total of 10 jumps per set. Do one to three sets.

INDEX
Numbers in **bold** refer to pages with illustrations